Nine Steps to Success

An ISO 27001:2013 Implementation Overview

North American edition

Nine Steps to Success

An ISO 27001:2013 Implementation Overview

North American edition

ALAN CALDER

IT Governance Publishing

Every possible effort has been made to ensure the information contained in this book is accurate at the time of going to press, and the publisher and the author cannot accept responsibility for any errors or omissions, however caused. Any opinions expressed in this book are those of the author, not the publisher. Websites identified are for reference only, not endorsement, and any website visits are at the reader's own risk. No responsibility for loss or damage occasioned to any person acting, or refraining from action, as a result of the material in this publication can be accepted by the publisher or the author.

Apart from any fair dealing for the purposes of research or private study, or criticism or review, as permitted under the Copyright, Designs and Patents Act 1988, this publication may only be reproduced, stored, or transmitted, in any form, or by any means, with the prior permission in writing of the publisher or, in the case of reprographic reproduction, in accordance with the terms of licenses issued by the Copyright Licensing Agency. Inquiries concerning reproduction outside those terms should be sent to the publisher at the following address:

IT Governance Publishing
IT Governance Limited
Unit 3, Clive Court
Bartholomew's Walk
Cambridgeshire Business Park
Ely, Cambridgeshire
CB7 4EA
United Kingdom

www.itgovernance.co.uk

The author has asserted the rights of the author under the Copyright, Designs and Patents Act, 1988, to be identified as the author of this work.

First published in the United Kingdom in 2005
by IT Governance Publishing: ISBN: 978-1-90535-612-6

Second edition published in 2013
ISBN: 978-1-84928-510-0

Third edition published in 2016
ISBN: 978-1-84928-823-1

North American edition published in 2017
ISBN: 978-1-84928-949-8

ABOUT THE AUTHOR

Alan Calder is the founder and executive chairman of IT Governance Ltd (*www.itgovernance.co.uk*), an information, advice and consultancy firm that helps company top managements tackle IT governance, risk management, compliance, and information security issues. He has many years of senior management experience in the private and public sectors.

The company operates websites around the world that distribute a range of books, tools, and other publications on IT governance, risk management, compliance, and information security.

In particular, our North American website, *www.itgovernanceusa.com*, is the gateway to a comprehensive range of ISO/IEC 27001 and cybersecurity products and services.

CONTENTS

Contents

Contents

INTRODUCTION

Cyber risk has become a critical business issue, with senior management increasingly under pressure—from customers, regulators, and partners—to ensure their organization can defend against, respond to, and recover from cyber attack.

Resilience against cyber attack requires an organization to defend itself across all of its attack surface: people, process, and technology. Significant investment in technological defenses are inadequate without at least commensurate investment in people and process; breaches in the people and process domains can be more devastating than those that come through inadequate technology. Effective cybersecurity therefore requires a comprehensive, systematic, and robust information security management system that encompasses people, process, and technology. Top managements, customers, and regulators all seek assurance that information risks have been identified and are being managed.

Impact of cyber breaches

Data breaches have measurable negative impacts on stock prices, customer retention, reputation, and profitability. Firms with better cybersecurity are usually able to recover more quickly from breaches than those without. Budgets, however, are tight and employees are continuously being pushed to take on more work. This means cybersecurity investments are often a 'grudge' investment—right up to the moment an organization suffers a cyber breach and it becomes obvious that the size of investment required to avoid the breach would have been considerably smaller than the scale of the financial and non-financial consequences of the breach itself.

Impact of regulation

While the United States currently has no single federal law that regulates cybersecurity and privacy throughout the country, several states do have their own cybersecurity laws in addition to their data breach notification laws1. There is a patchwork of industry-specific federal laws (such as HIPAA and GLBA) and state legislation whose scope and jurisdiction vary. The NYDFS Cybersecurity and Massachusetts regulations are examples of state cybersecurity regulations. Outside of the US, many countries are introducing cybersecurity laws—including China. In addition, organizations providing services in the EU must now also comply with the EU General Data Protection Regulation—breaches of which could bring regulatory penalties of up to 4% of global revenues. Therefore, the challenge of compliance for organizations that conduct business across all 50 states and potentially across the world is considerable.

What organizations really need is some form of silver bullet that, at a stroke, brings cost-effective compliance with legislation and regulation, together with enhanced cyber resilience and market competitiveness. While silver bullets do not exist, of course, ISO/IEC 27001 is an international standard that comes closest to performing this function in the cybersecurity environment.

---

[1] *www.itgovernanceusa.com/data-breach-notification-laws#C1*

ISO/IEC 27001

The international standard ISO/IEC 27001:2013 *Information technology – Security techniques – Information security management systems – Requirements* is the blueprint for managing information security in line with an organization's business, contractual and regulatory requirements, and its risk appetite. Information security has always been an international issue, and this version of the Standard reflects eight years of improvements in the understanding of effective information security management. It also takes account of the evolution in the cyber threat landscape over that period and allows for a wide range of best-practice controls.

Information security is now clearly also a management issue, a governance responsibility. The design and implementation of an information security management system (ISMS) is a management role, not a technological one. It requires the full range of managerial skills and attributes, from project management and prioritization through communication, sales skills, and motivation, to delegation, monitoring, and discipline. A good manager who has no technological background or insight can lead a successful ISMS implementation, but without management skills, the most technologically sophisticated information security expert will fail at the task.

This is particularly the case if the organization wants to derive the maximum long-term business value from the implementation of an ISMS. Achieving external certification is increasingly a standard cost of doing business; achieving the level of information security awareness and good internal practice that enables an organization to safely surf the stormy, cruel seas of the information age requires a level of culture change no less profound than that required to shift from industrial to post-industrial operations.

I know all this because my background is as a general manager, not as a technologist. I came to information security in 1995 because I was concerned about the information security exposures faced by the company of which I was CEO. When you're the CEO, and you're interested in it, you can make an ISMS happen—as I've proved a number of times. While this book will shorten the learning curve for other CEOs in my position, really it is aimed at the manager—often an IT or information security manager, sometimes a quality manager—who is charged with tackling an ISO 27001 implementation and wants to understand the route to a positive outcome. It builds on the experience of many ISO 27001 implementations and reflects the nine-step implementation methodology that now underpins all the ISO 27001 products and services accessible through IT Governance Ltd (*www.itgovernanceusa.com*), the company I founded back in 2005. These nine steps work in any organization—public sector, voluntary sector, or private—anywhere in the world. Technology infrastructure, business model, organizational architecture, and regulatory requirements all inform the context for implementation of an ISO 27001 ISMS, but do not limit its applicability. We've helped implement an ISO 27001 ISMS in businesses with as few as two people, in mammoth, multi-national global enterprises, and in organizations of all sizes and types in between.

The second-biggest challenge that, in my experience, is faced by information security technologists everywhere in the world is getting—and keeping—the C-suite's attention. The biggest challenge is gaining—and maintaining—the organization's *interest in* and *application to* the project.

Ongoing press and public attention regarding cyber risk is driving the issue onto top management agendas and, when top managements do finally understand they need to act—systematically and comprehensively—against information security threats, they become very interested in hearing from their information security specialists. They even develop an appetite for investing organizational dollars into hardware and software solutions, and for mandating the development of a new ISMS—or the tightening up of an existing one.

A successful ISMS project stems from and depends on genuine top management support. Progress is quicker if the project is seen as having a credible business need: to win an outsourcing or other customer contract, for instance, or to comply with a public funding requirement, improve competitiveness, or reduce regulatory compliance costs and exposures.

When we first decided to tackle information security way back in 1995, my organization in the UK was required to achieve ISO 9001 certification as a condition of its branding and trading license. We also intended to sell information security and environmental management services and—out of a desire to practice what we preached, as well as from a determination to achieve the identifiable benefits of tackling all these components of our business—we decided to pursue both BS 7799 and ISO 14001 at the same time.

BS 7799 certification only existed then in an unaccredited form and was, essentially, a Code of Practice. There was only one part to it and, while certification was technically not possible, some certification bodies were interested in issuing statements of conformity. The other standards we were interested in did all exist, but at that time it was generally expected an organization would approach each standard individually, developing standalone manuals and processes. This was hardly surprising, as it was unusual for any organization to pursue more than one standard at any time.

We made the momentous decision to approach the issue from primarily a business perspective, rather than a quality one. We decided we wanted to create a single, integrated management system that would work for our business, and was capable of achieving multiple certifications. While this seemed to fly in the face of standard practice around management system implementation, it seemed to be completely in line with the spirit of the standards themselves.

We also decided we wanted everyone in the organization to take part in the process of creating and developing the integrated management system we envisioned. We believed this was the fastest and most certain way of getting them to become real contributors to the project, both in the short and long term. We used external consultants for part of the ISO 9001 project, but there simply was no BS 7799 expertise available externally.

This lack of BS 7799 experts was a minor challenge compared with the lack of useful books or tools. Today, you can purchase books such as *An Introduction to Information Security and ISO 27001:2013*[2]; however, back then there were bookshelves full of thick, technologically focused books on all sorts of information security issues, but nothing that might tell a business manager how to systematically implement an ISMS. We had no option but to try to work it out for ourselves.

---

[2] *www.itgovernanceusa.com/shop/product/an-introduction-to-information-security-and-iso-27001-2013-a-pocket-guide-second-edition*

Introduction

We actually did the job two times: once under the unaccredited scheme and the second after the Standard had become a two-parter and was accredited (the earlier, single part had become a Code of Practice, while a new part—a specification for an ISMS—had been introduced). In fact, our accredited audit was also our certification body's first observed audit for its own formal accreditation. While that was an interesting experience, it did mean our systems had to be particularly robust if they were to stand the simultaneous scrutiny of two levels of external auditors.

We underwent external examination on five separate occasions within a few months, and our integrated management system achieved all the required external certifications and recognitions. We did this without anything more than the part-time assistance of one ISO 9001 consultant and an internal quality management team of one. Steve Watkins, now a director of IT Governance Ltd and a UKAS Technical Assessor for ISO 27001, was that quality manager, and he did most of the real work to create our integrated, multi-standard management system. Admittedly, the organization was a relatively small one, but although we only employed about 80 people (across three sites), we did also have an associate consultant team that was nearly 100 strong. And back then, we probably could not have done something as complex as this in a much larger organization.

The lessons Steve and I learned in our first two implementations—and our experience with ISO 27001 implementations since then, often in very substantial public and private sector organizations around the world—has enabled us to crystallize the nine key steps to a successful ISMS implementation.

Properly managed and led, any ISO 27001 project can be successful. We've proved it.

Over the years, my organization, IT Governance Ltd, has developed approaches to implementing an ISMS that can help project managers identify and overcome many of the very real problems they face in achieving a successful outcome. We've worked successfully with organizations in North America, the UK and Europe, and across the rest of the world. We've also developed unique tools and techniques that simplify the process, that fit together around the nine steps described in this book, and that enable organizations to succeed without additional external assistance. Information security success, in the long term, does not need to be consultant-dependent; but it does depend on the organization itself. This book describes the key issues—the building blocks of success—and tells you how to tackle them.

The book is intended to be a fairly high-level guide to the nine-step implementation process and it therefore refers, from time to time, to more detailed books or tools that have been developed or published by my company. In particular, it often makes reference to the substantially more detailed and comprehensive *IT Governance – An International Guide to Data Security and ISO27001/ISO27002, Sixth Edition*[3], which Steve and I originally wrote to fill the evident gap in available guidance on the subject. That book is also now the Open University's postgraduate text book on information security.

In each case where I make a specific reference, the book or tool is unique and was developed to do the specific job I

---

[3] *www.itgovernanceusa.com/shop/product/it-governance-an-international-guide-to-data-security-and-iso27001iso27002-sixth-edition*

describe it as doing. We developed these books, tools, and services because there simply was nothing available on the market that did a comparable job or that delivered the sort of return on investment we know our customers are looking for.

The ISO 27000 family

The information security Standard is, in fact, a two-part standard that has evolved considerably. One part of the Standard (ISO 27001:2013) provides a specification for the ISMS (it uses words like 'shall', particularly in Annex A, which is the list of controls). The other part (ISO 27002:2013) has the status of a Code of Practice: the assembled guidance on best-practice information security from around the world.

The difference between a specification and a Code of Practice, in the world of management systems standards, is a specification contains the word 'shall' and specifies what is mandatory for a system if it is to comply with the standard, while a Code of Practice provides guidance and uses words like 'should' to indicate compliance is not mandatory. Organizations can choose controls from this Code of Practice or anywhere else, provided the requirements of the specification are met. Accredited certification takes place against a requirements specification, not a Code of Practice.

ISO 27001 is linked to ISO 27002 and, where the organization uses the Annex A controls, ISO 27002 provides the guidance on how to implement those controls.

These two standards are supported by ISO 27000, which provides the definitions on which they rely. This is a lightweight work, but contains useful guidance and all the essential definitions that will help ensure everyone involved in the implementation project is on the same page.

You need to obtain, and study, copies of both *ISO/IEC 27001:2013* and *ISO/IEC 27002:2013*. It is against ISO 27001 specifically that compliance is measured and the exact words in that Standard have precedence over any other guidance or commentary. Copies of the Standards are obtainable from your national standards body or from *www.itgovernanceusa.com* (IT Governance Ltd is an authorized standards distributor for a number of standards bodies).

In cases of doubt or uncertainty, your certification auditor will refer to the Standards for clarification; if everything you do can be tied down to specific words in the Standard, you will be in a strong position. On the other hand, do not assume your action is incorrect if you do something the Standard does not specify. The Standard is a *minimum* requirement, not a maximum one.

Links to other standards

ISO 27001 is supported by a family of related best-practice standards, each of which provides additional guidance on a specific aspect of information security management. This family of standards is continuously growing and developing; up-to-date information is available from *www.itgovernanceusa.com/iso27000-family*.

ISO 27001:2013 harmonizes with ISO 9001:2015 and ISO 14001:2015, as well as with ISO 22301, ISO 20000-1, and ISO 50001, so management systems can be effectively integrated.

Introduction

ISO 27001 implicitly recognizes information security and an ISMS should form an integrated part of any internal control system created as part of corporate governance procedures. The Standard fits in with the approach required, for instance, under Sarbanes–Oxley, for risk management.

There is further discussion on the relationships with these other standards, more detail on the interrelationship with ISO 27002, and initial guidance on how frameworks such as ITIL (and ISO 20000) and COBIT could be used in an ISO 27001 implementation in *An Introduction to Information Security and ISO27001*[4].

Before you start

It's worth getting appropriate training before you start your ISMS project.

The most useful training courses are those that provide an introduction to the whole subject, those that cover implementation, and those that cover audit. All good courses are accredited by an external examination board, such as the International Board for IT Governance Qualifications (IBITGQ—*www.ibitgq.org*).

An ISO 27001 ISMS Foundation Course is a one-day course that provides a broad awareness of the subject and is suitable for all project team members.

An ISO 27001 Lead Implementer Course is the ideal course for those who will be responsible for taking the project forward. This is a three-day course that provides practical guidance on effective implementation. The Certified

---

[4] *www.itgovernanceusa.com/shop/product/an-introduction-to-information-security-and-iso-27001-2013-a-pocket-guide-second-edition*

Information Security Lead Implementer (CIS LI) qualification is widely recognized, and CIS LI courses and exams reflect the nine-step approach I describe.

All management systems must be subject to internal (management) audit. A Lead ISMS (or, possibly, an Internal ISMS) Auditor Course provides those inside your organization who will be charged with designing and managing your internal information security audit process with the skills they need to do this effectively.

You can see more detailed information about these and other courses here: *www.itgovernanceusa.com/training*. These qualifications can be achieved by attending either a classroom (daily travel or accommodation expenses) or a live online (make your own drinks and meals) course.

Training will also, of course, be an important facilitator of the types of changes your organization may need to make in terms of information security management. Exposing the whole project team to the principles of ISO 27001 through an ISO 27001 Foundation training course is a sensible step after you provide for the critical lead implementer and lead auditor training. Staff throughout the business will also need specific training in those aspects of security policy that will affect their day-to-day work. The IT manager and IT staff will all need specific competencies in Information Security (see ISO 27001, Clause 7.2) and, if they need to be enhanced, it should be delivered by an organization that recognizes and understands the technical aspects of ISO 27001 training. You can find more information about appropriate training here:

www.itgovernanceusa.com/training.

CHAPTER 1: PROJECT MANDATE

It may be something of a cliché, but for information security management system (ISMS) projects, it is certainly true to say that well begun is half-way done. The person charged with leading an ISO/IEC 27001:2013 ISMS project has to reduce something that looks potentially complex, difficult, and expensive in terms of time and resources, to something that everyone believes can be achieved in the timeframe allocated and with the resources allowed. And then you have to make sure it is actually delivered!

What this actually means is the ISMS project leader has to set up the project in such a way that it is adequately resourced, there is enough time (including for everything that may go wrong), and everyone understands the risks in the project and accepts the controls that are being deployed to minimize them.

Almost everyone dislikes change; very few people relish dealing with the unknown. Most people will see an ISMS project as something that brings both change and the unknown into their working life, and not everyone will welcome it. That's normal—they'll get on board in the end.

The project leader, in the first phase of the project, is the person to whom everyone else in the organization turns for insight, comfort, and support. You have to be the person who provides enthusiasm, certainty, and an understanding of what is involved.

This means learning on the job in a transparent fashion is not advisable. I don't mean you need to know all the answers at the outset—that is not realistic. As long as you have a clear understanding of the strategic issues and practical knowledge of where to turn for advice and guidance, you can be effective—even if you're only a day or two ahead of everyone else in the detailed knowledge required for the project.

You'd be surprised at the number of times someone has kicked off an ISMS project without adequate preparation, has failed to answer a series of questions or challenges about specific issues adequately, and has then been surprised that the project has lost credibility rather quickly.

Your CEO's support for the project is even more important than your own understanding of what you're trying to achieve. Information security is both a management and a governance issue. Successful implementation of an ISMS depends absolutely on the project having real support from the top of the organization. With it, you have a real shot at success; without it, none at all. *Securing real top management support*—not mere lip service—is key to ISO 27001 success. In this context, I'm not necessarily talking about the CEO of a large, multi-subsidiary organization; I'm talking about the person who is accountable for the business success or failure of the trading entity considering adopting ISO 27001. This could be a trading division, a subsidiary company, a standalone unit, or a virtual organization.

It is important to be clear about the meaning of 'accountable' in this context. I am talking about the person whose job and career ultimately depend on the success of the business entity that is considering ISO 27001; this person does not always occupy the role that is formally 'where the buck stops.' All organizations know exactly where the buck really stops, and this is the person I refer to as the CEO in this chapter.

Strategic alignment

The first reason the CEO must fully support you and the ISMS project is it is a business project, not an IT project. It must be fully aligned with the business model, business strategy, and goals, and has to be a priority for the business and be allocated an appropriate level of resources. While the CEO is unlikely to be the ISMS project leader, the only person who can effectively prioritize cybersecurity is the CEO. No single project leader is in a position to be clear about the organization's strategic needs and goals, but as this is a strategic project that affects everyone, you need to be 'in the loop' so you can tailor your own plans to deliver the organization's business priorities.

You also need to know what the strategic risks faced by the organization are, and how these are reflected and prioritized in information security risks. There are many possible questions, the answers to which will be critical to your approach and detailed plan. For instance, is the risk of intellectual property theft more significant—with a greater potential impact—than the risk of, for example, a three-day business closure? Is regulatory compliance more, or less, important than reducing the cost of sales? Is information security and regulatory compliance going to be important in outsourcing solutions (or, when faced with a choice between a lower cost but less secure, and a more secure but more expensive outsourcing option, which one will the organization choose)? How should conflict between the regulatory requirements of two different jurisdictions in which the organization trades be resolved? What is the trade-off between the operational flexibility allowed to subsidiary organizations, and implementation of a minimum, consistent level of information security and IT service reliability? What are the long-term plans for specific support services (if they're to be outsourced, then you're going to approach ISMS implementation differently than if they're staying in-house)? There are many such questions, the answers to which you need to know before you even start planning. And there are many others that will come up in the course of the project.

Prioritization and endorsement

The second reason you require this level of support is that, without it, the project simply will not happen. It is not enough for the CEO and executive management simply to acknowledge the project is important. It is not enough that they merely talk about it. It is not enough that you know the organization's strategic priorities and are able to align the project with the business plan.

If it really is to happen, senior management must be committed, well and truly determined to achieve it. Top management commitment means the project gets the financial and human resources it needs. It gets the oversight, 'face time' and internal communication headlines it needs. Unless you have this sort of commitment, there will be lots of things people throughout the organization will see as higher priorities than your project. Of course, there are going to be *some* higher priorities; what you need is clear prioritization that is understood across the business and is continuously supported by the CEO.

The relative prioritization of your project must be clearly understood. Within that context, it needs to have the firm and uncompromising endorsement of the CEO. By 'endorsement' I mean that, when those occasionally unnecessary internal barriers appear, the words: "This is a project endorsed/mandated by the CEO" should go a long way to overcoming them.

Change management

The third reason you need the CEO's support is an ISMS project is likely to be a change management project. The implementation of an ISMS is not a low-impact activity. It may require changes to how computer users do a number of things and it also affects aspects of managers' everyday activities. A successful ISMS project is, in other words, a low-key but nevertheless wide-ranging change management project, and the way you approach it has to learn from the experience of successful change management programs.

There have been many books written about change management. Many of these projects fail to deliver the benefits used to justify the expense of commencing and seeing them through. Successful implementation of an ISMS does not require a detailed, strategic change management program, particularly not one devised and driven by external consultants. What it does require is complete clarity among senior management, those charged with driving the project forward, and those whose work practices will be affected as to why the change is necessary, what the end result must look like, and why this result is essential. For this reason you want your CEO to be leading by example, doing all the things you're going to want everyone else to be doing.

The fact is the Standard itself demands this level of support. It will not allow any certification body to certify an ISMS without firm evidence senior management is committed. The reason for this is simple: if commitment is lacking, the ISMS will not be adequate; the risks to the organization will not have been properly recognized or fully addressed; and the strategic business goals and consequent future information security requirements are unlikely to have been considered.

The CEO's role

Ideally, the CEO should be the driving force behind the program, and achievement of ISO 27001 certification should be a clearly stated goal in the current business plan. The CEO needs to understand fully the strategic issues around IT governance and information security, and the value to the company of successful certification. The CEO must be able to articulate this to the directors and top management, and to deal with objections and issues arising. Above all, he or she must be sufficiently in command of this part of the business plan to be able to keep it on track against its strategic goals.

The chairperson and top management should give as much attention to monitoring progress against the ISO 27001 implementation plan as they do to monitoring all other key business goals. Clause 5.1 of the Standard specifically requires evidence of this commitment from the top: "Top management shall demonstrate leadership and commitment with respect to the information security management system." If the CEO, chairperson, and board of directors are not behind this project, there is little point in proceeding; certification will not happen without clear evidence of such commitment. This principle of leadership from the top is, of course, also essential to all major change projects.

If you are already the CEO of the organization, then you're doing exactly the right thing by reading this book and preparing to drive the information security project yourself. If you're not the CEO, then you have to secure the sort of commitment and support I described above.

The ideal leader of an ISMS project is a business leader—a chief operations officer (COO) or a line of business leader. Adopting an ISMS is a business project and business leadership is therefore fundamental to its success. ISMS projects often fail because they have been set up apparently as a technology initiative and are therefore seen and treated as narrow and undeserving of full business commitment. 'Just another IT project' is the wrong message for driving an ISMS into the culture of the organization.

There are, of course, organizations in which the chief information officer (CIO) is a member of the senior management team, responsible for an integrated function that includes information security, and already has the full trust and support of the CEO and top management. In such an organization the CIO could be the driver of the project, but it will still need the CEO's commitment and support, not least so everyone in the organization understands that securing recognition is a business priority. The CIO will also urgently need to build a cross-business project team. I will return to this later.

The project mandate

The project mandate is where you capture initial evidence of this commitment in a usable format. A project mandate (laid out in a project initiation document—PID) is a document that is widely used to capture the key elements of any complex project. It ensures there is a single, original point of reference that sets out the three keys to project success: deliverables, timeline, and budget.

Complex projects fail because one or more of these three project variables are poorly identified and/or managed. 'Scope creep' is one of the most common roots of project failure. Project mandates, therefore, seek to clearly identify project scope and to pin down the three variables in order to support an effective project governance process.

Your project mandate should address these four points:

1. Deliverables: Identify the objective as the achievement of ISO 27001 certification for either a specific part or the whole of the organization and, if possible, identify why information security is important for your organization.

2. Timeline: Create an outline project plan and identify a target completion date on the basis of the nine steps to success.

3. Budget: Identify the resources, both internal and external, as well as the training, software, and tools you will need for the project.

4. Authorization to proceed: The mandate should contain management endorsement of the project and authorization to proceed, in order to achieve the identified objectives using the budgeted resources.

Deliverables and the project objective

While the project deliverable is relatively easy to define (for example, achieve ISO 27001 certification within four months), you still need to be clear about the reasons for pursuing that objective as well as clarifying the difference between project objective and information security objectives.

The purpose of an ISMS is, of course, to reduce and control risks to your information. The actual objective (or objectives) of your ISMS project may be different to the purposes of the ISMS itself, and you should be clear about these differences if you are to appropriately focus both the project and the ISMS. The project objective may be, for instance, to secure ISO 27001 certification within a given timeframe in order to meet a contractual or regulatory requirement, to improve business competitiveness, or to reduce the cost and complexity of sales and marketing responses to tender invitations. Project objectives, in other words, link specifically to business benefits that are to be derived from their achievement. Project objectives will usually be high level and performance against them should be easy to track.

Information security objectives may be, but are not necessarily, related to the project objectives. Information security objectives will definitely be linked to the preservation of confidentiality, integrity, and availability of information within the context of the organization and in relation to its risk appetite. Progress toward achieving information security objectives must be measurable, which means the objectives themselves need to be specific, measurable, achievable, realistic, and time-bound. Typical objectives might, for instance, be to reduce the number of disruptive information security incidents from 14 per year to 2 per year, or to increase network availability from 97% and $20\times7\times360$ to 99.99999% and $24\times7\times365$. Such objectives will be broken down into lower level objectives, with accountability for their achievement allocated to appropriate departments and levels within the organization.

Gap analysis

Most organizations are already taking steps to manage their information security. While there may be significant vulnerabilities, it is not as though nothing is currently being done! The starting point for your project is usually, therefore, to understand how far your current practices are from the requirements set out in ISO 27001, and the best way to do this is with what we call a 'gap analysis.' This is a quick, reasonably high-level audit of your current information security management practices against the requirements set out in ISO 27001, which identifies where there is a shortfall and also identifies what resources and capabilities you have in place for closing the gap, or what resources you might need to bring in from outside. If you have already defined information security objectives, your gap analysis could also identify what steps still need to be taken in order to achieve those objectives.

You might call the output from the gap analysis a security improvement plan (SIP). This SIP becomes, in effect, your ISMS Project Plan.

Budget and resources

You cannot implement an ISO 27001 ISMS on your own, or without some investment in tools and training. For ISO 27001, 'resources' means human, technical, information, and financial resources. Purpose-designed tools are likely to reduce project time, error, and cost. The two most useful tools are documentation templates and risk assessment software. The risk assessment solution we most recommend is available directly from Vigilant Software, here: *www.vigilantsoftware.co.uk*.

A number of people across the organization, and from different levels within it, will need to contribute. You may also want to bring in external consultants, whether for guidance or because you need additional resources to execute your project plan.

There are a number of specialist areas in which consultants can be helpful:

- You can use consultants—trusted third parties—to communicate the seriousness of the information risks faced by the organization and the need, therefore, for an ISMS.

- You can use consultants to provide advice on specific (most often technical) issues—for instance, scoping and how external or internal threats might affect your decisions about project scope—to carry out a risk assessment, to deal with documentation, or to advise on integration with other management systems.

- You can (and might be well advised to) use consultants to help you identify appropriate technical controls for specific risks. This holds true as long as the consultants have no financial interest in any solutions they might recommend and fully understand and can help you apply the two key financial measures of return on investment (ROI) and total cost of ownership (TCO) to any solutions they propose.

- You can use consultants in a mentoring capacity, to review critical documents, and as a sounding board with whom you can discuss key steps in your project and key issues you have to deal with, and possible solutions.

You do not need to hire external consultants in order to achieve ISO 27001. Many organizations get the job done completely without any outside assistance. Many others simply do not have the time or resources to structure, manage, and deliver an ISMS project without additional input. Whether or not you hire consultants is, therefore, dependent on resource availability, budget, and your organization's cultural preference for working things out for itself versus bringing in outside expertise.

The major benefits of using outside consultants should be that:

- Even if they are only working on your project one day per week, their time with you is focused exclusively on your project, and
- They have significant ISO 27001 implementation experience, which should help you avoid blind alleys, over-detailed or impractical methodologies, disjointed implementations, or losing track entirely.

If you use consultants, it should go without saying they are able to point at substantial experience implementing ISO 27001 and, of course, they themselves are ISO 27001 certified.

The 'do-it-yourself' approach can be simplified and accelerated by using the kinds of established tools and techniques discussed in this book, and by following this nine-step methodology.

The output from your gap analysis is therefore an ideal starting point for determining the resource requirements of the project, starting with whether or not you intend to use external consultants or will be recruiting for key internal ISMS or project roles. It is particularly useful to identify who will be needed on the ISMS project team (we'll discuss this shortly); who will be invited to contribute from across the business; who will have the key project roles and responsibilities; who owns the project; who the project reports to internally; how progress is tracked and reported; etc.

The major benefit of identifying your resource requirements in your PID is that, once top management have signed off on the project, you should be able to rely on having access to those resources. In any organization where a considerable part of the required resource has other duties and responsibilities, this is a major benefit.

Those involved with the ISMS will need to be competent to carry out their roles. I'll return to the issue of competence later, but you will need to start taking steps to acquire competent personnel right away.

Apart from training and skill development, resource requirements may also include software, toolkits, staff awareness eLearning, training, and/or consultancy support. Each of those options will be addressed at appropriate points in this book.

Timeline and outline project plan

Your gap analysis should also enable you to create an outline project plan, most sensibly in the form of a Gantt chart. At this stage, it can be quite high level, setting out timelines, milestones, and key objectives. Of course, the end point of your project plan should be the achievement of your project objective within the planned project timeframe; your information security objectives likely will be pursued and achieved over much longer timeframes.

As your project planning becomes more detailed, so will your Gantt chart; you will, however, still want to stay within the original timelines and avoid disruptions to the project that could impact on the timeline you commit to achieving.

Project initiation document

A project initiation document (PID) is a document most commonly used within a formal IT project management environment. However, the concept applies just as well to any complex project that involves multiple contributors, a number of whom may have multiple roles both inside and outside of the project. It is also an excellent way to record project objectives clearly and to have the key initial components of the project approved by top management.

If your organization already has a process that meets these needs, you should use it. The sooner the ISMS project can be evidently set within your business-as-usual arrangements, the better. If you do not already have such a process, you can either create one yourself, or simply purchase the PID toolkit from one of our websites.

Within your document management system, the PID should be treated as a record; after all, that is what it is!

CHAPTER 2: PROJECT INITIATION

The project mandate is the first step in getting your information security management system (ISMS) project off the ground. The second step is to set up the project itself and the project governance structure, effectively an extension of what is contained in the project initiation document (PID). The project governance structure needs to be more elaborate for complex, lengthy projects than for quick, relatively straightforward ones.

The project governance structure will consist of:

- The project objective
- The project team, typically with a project board for projects scheduled to take longer than nine months
- A project plan (who, when) that is a more detailed version of the high-level project plan included with the PID, including scheduled review dates, and
- A project risk register.

Objectives

The project and information security objectives will feed into the information security policy and will start to inform the ISO 27001 requirements around monitoring, measurement, analysis and evaluation, and management review. It will include a time-bound statement regarding achievement of either certification or compliance to the Standard, as applicable, plus the definition of high-level information security objectives.

Project management

As part of putting together the PID, you should already have determined who the project owner will be and, if possible, who will chair the project team/working group. At this point, you ideally start creating a RACI matrix for the project. This identifies who is Responsible, Accountable, Consulted, and Informed regarding key project decisions and each of the information security management processes as they are drawn up.

The project team should be made up of roles that have responsibility for representing the interests of every key part of the organization. This does not mean every part of the organization must be directly represented, as that might create a huge and unwieldy team, but each person on the team should be aware of whose interests they need to look out for. There should also be a spread of levels of seniority, with delegated authority from the respective manager(s).

Project leadership

Unless the CEO is personally leading the project, you should ask for active support, specifically requesting that the CEO:

- Makes a point of understanding the business benefits of pursuing an information security strategy, and the return on investment (more on this below) this project will achieve for the organization.

- Leads a presentation (which you will prepare) on the information security strategy to the board of directors and top management, includes ISMS certification in the organization's business goals for the year, secures board support for the objective expressed in the project mandate, and arranges for ongoing board monitoring of project progress throughout its life (which will ensure the project achieves and maintains the sort of political profile that will improve its chances of success).

- Personally leads presentations (which you prepare) on the project to the executive or senior management of the organization as well as to all staff in each of the organizational forums that are used for staff communication.

- Nominates his or her most senior business line executive to support the project and lead the steering group (more on which below), to provide day-to-day backing and support for you, and to lead the change management effort. This individual has to be personally committed to the success of the project, prepared to do whatever is necessary to succeed.

- Clearly sets out—for senior management and for everyone in the organization—the prioritization for this project and your authority to seek the input and involvement of all whose contribution will be essential to your success.

- Sets a personal example of applying all the work practices and following all the procedures that will become part of the new ISMS.

Senior management support

Senior management support is equally important. An ISMS project ranges across all parts of the organization so you need to be sure all key leaders are on message. Of course, there will always be varying degrees of enthusiasm for an ISMS project and not all of the senior management will be as enthusiastic as you would like them to be. There are two important steps in securing the support you will need from this group:

1. Set up a cross-organizational steering group to drive the project forward. This steering group should be led either by the CEO or by the CEO's nominated deputy, and should be primarily a business-oriented group. In other words, it should consist primarily of business managers who have a direct personal interest in the effectiveness of any ISMS project and whose contribution will ensure the ISMS meets business needs and becomes a fully functional part of the organization. This group should include any individuals likely to resist the project and, if possible, those individuals should be given responsibilities key to the success of the project. If this is unlikely to work, pursue alternate methods of isolating them—this is one area in which a committed CEO should be asked to provide personal input.

I cannot stress enough how important it is for this group not to have a preponderance of IT or technical people—the project must be seen as a business project, not an IT one. This group might, depending on the size of the organization, be the project group. In larger organizations, the steering group will be responsible for 'operationalizing' the approved plan for implementation of an ISMS, delegating detailed work to a project group, and monitoring progress on a regular basis. Members of the steering group should also be barred from sending junior members of their teams in their place. Finally, keep in mind steering groups should be small; between three and seven people is the optimum range for effective oversight and decision-making.

2. The CEO should make the initial presentation to the steering group. This presentation should focus on information security risks and the potential impact of a failure to implement proper security throughout the organization, and should set out the relative prioritization and importance the project has. It should be clear to everyone in the steering group that this project carries the CEO's personal endorsement, and it will receive high-level oversight throughout its life.

Project team

In large organizations, the dual-level management structure described above might be appropriate, with a management steering group and an executive project team. The steering group would be responsible for strategy, project governance, and ISMS oversight. The executive team, meanwhile, would be responsible for designing, implementing, and operating the ISMS. In smaller organizations, the functions of both groups are typically embedded in a single project group. Either or both of these groups might have the characteristics of what is often called a 'cross-functional forum.'

This project group, or team, should be drawn from those parts of the organization most likely to be affected by the implementation of the ISMS. A *very small* number of functional experts, including HR/personnel, should also be involved. The balance is important; a properly functioning ISMS depends on everyone in the business understanding and applying its controls and, if the project team is made up of a preponderance of non-technical people, it is more likely to produce something everyone in the business understands. The team should certainly include at least one experienced project manager, who will be responsible for tracking and reporting progress against the planned objectives.

The project team should report directly to either the chair of the steering group or (preferably) the CEO and should have the appropriate delegated authority to implement the mandated ISMS project plan. Clauses 7.1 and 7.2 of ISO 27001 require, between them, the provision of adequate and competent resources to establish, maintain, and continually improve the ISMS, and putting an appropriately structured project team in place is the first step in doing so.

Project team members should be selected from those in senior positions across the organization. Key functions that should be represented are quality/process management, human resources, training, and IT and facilities management, as they will all have to change their working practices significantly as a result of the decision to implement an ISMS. Apart from the manager responsible for information security and a trained information security expert, the most critical representation will be from sales, operations, and administration. Obviously, non-sales organizations (public sector and non-profits, for instance) have units that work with stakeholders and these should also be involved. The functions in which the majority of the organization's personnel are employed are the ones that will be most affected by the implementation of an ISMS. Ideally, the people invited to represent these functions should be among the most senior and widely respected individuals within them.

As mentioned earlier in this book, the change process ISO 27001 implementation will require has a cultural impact. It is critical those most able to represent and articulate the needs and concerns of the key parts of the organization are included in the working party. Without their involvement, there is unlikely to be the buy-in necessary for the ISMS to be effectively developed and implemented.

Project team chair

The choice of chair for the project team is usually critical to its success, both as a group and in terms of how the rest of the organization views and responds to it. The chair needs, therefore, to be someone who is capable of commanding the respect of all members of the project team. They need to be wholly committed to achieving the goal of a certified ISMS within the agreed timetable. They need to be pragmatic and prepared to think outside the box in identifying solutions to organizational problems that are affecting implementation.

The chair should not be from any one of the organization's support functions, as this will usually brand the project as unimportant. An IT person should on no account lead the team, as the implementation of an ISMS simply cannot afford to be seen only as an IT project. Preferably, the chair should have a broad managerial responsibility within the organization as well as experience in implementing cross-organizational change projects. Ideally, they will be the CEO or the C-suite member responsible for implementation of the corporate security policy.

In smaller organizations, this person might also be the manager responsible for information security (described below). In larger organizations where this is likely a full-time role, the manager responsible for information security should properly report to the chair of the steering group or the CEO.

Not only is the structure outlined here the most effective method for delivery of the ISMS, it is also very clear evidence of commitment to its implementation from the very top of the organization. The external ISO 27001 auditor will expect to see such evidence.

Information security manager

Whatever you decide about the use of consultants, you will need to appoint an information security manager. It is good sense for one manager to be responsible for all security-related activities—both strategic and day-to-day—within the organization. If this person is appointed before the steering group and/or project team is set up, their brief could include the formation of these teams. The benefit of this route is speed and, potentially, simplicity. The C-suite member charged with the responsibility for ensuring implementation of the ISMS could simply select and appoint an appropriate person, who could then get on with putting together an appropriate project team, which would then take things forward. By contrast, the selection and training of the members of the steering group is potentially more time consuming and the period during which they are learning their roles will precede the point at which they are competent to select and appoint an appropriate manager. The organization may not wish to pursue this slower route.

While the information security manager does not need to be the same person who is appointed as the organization's information security expert (the skill sets required for the managerial role, particularly in a larger organization, may be different from those required for the security expert's role), this person will still need adequate training in information security matters. Obviously, the person selected for the managerial role will need to be an effective manager, with well-developed communication and project management skills.

Experience suggests ISO 27001 projects work best when the organization gives a single person the responsibility for ensuring the ISMS meets the requirements of the Standard, and for reporting to top management on the performance of the ISMS. While two separate individuals could hold these roles, the information security manager could potentially undertake both.

Specialist information security advice

Information security has a number of technical aspects and many technical considerations must be taken into account when designing and implementing an ISMS. As I said earlier, this does not mean the project should be led by a technologist, or have anything other than a complete business focus. The organization does need to have an available source of specialist information security advice, who can provide, when required, detailed input on information security threats, appropriate control configurations, and reliable monitoring and auditing processes. This role can be difficult to fill on a part-time basis—you will want your specialist to have a working and detailed knowledge of your organization—but not all organizations can afford a full-time resource. This leaves two alternatives, both of which involve substantial training: appoint someone from within the IT team to the role, and ensure they are adequately trained on the information security issues, or appoint someone from elsewhere—possibly, in a small organization, the information security manager—and ensure they have adequate technical training and depth of know-how. The choice between the two options will be a pragmatic one, informed by the characters, attributes, and personal circumstances of the potential candidates.

In larger organizations, of course, the recruitment and appointment of such an expert should be a priority. The one area in which such a person likely will lack experience is the information security management Standard and, therefore, steps should be taken to provide this person with specific ISMS training such as that provided by an IBITGQ ATO (International Board for IT Governance Qualifications Accredited Training Organization).

Functional specialists

There are a number of functional specialists who you will want involved in the project and whose contributions will need to be effectively inspired and coordinated. These people include the leaders of the IT unit, the head of HR, the risk assessment or risk management experts within the organization, the premises security people, and both the finance and internal audit teams. It is worth seeking their early involvement by including them in the initial rounds of briefings on the need for an ISMS, eliciting their views on risks and threats, and considering their likely critical contributions.

While you should involve them early on—because with them you will succeed, whereas without them you are almost certain to fail—keep in mind and be sure they fully understand this is a business project, one that will be led by and reflect the needs of the business.

Project plan

For a long time, planning has been seen as an essential precursor to project success. Of course, while it is necessary, it is not sufficient—a well-planned project can still fail for any one of a number of reasons. At the highest level, ISMS project planning means dealing successfully with all the issues identified in this book; each of the nine steps is also a critical component of a successful ISMS project plan. At a more practical level, planning is essential to ISO 27001 success. For the purposes of an ISMS implementation, 'planning' includes dealing with issues like the deployment of consultants, how the project will be managed, how different management systems will be integrated, and the identification of key responsibilities and resource requirements throughout the project life cycle.

Anyone taking on an ISO 27001 project should, once the organization decides to go ahead, obtain and read *IT Governance – An International Guide to Data Security and ISO27001/ISO27002*, Sixth Edition[5]. The book is unique, and provides comprehensive and detailed advice on most of the issues you will encounter in implementing an ISMS. The advice in this overview book is consistent with, and dovetails very directly into, the contents of *An International Guide to Data Security and ISO27001/ISO27002*.

Just as helpfully, ISO 27001 is designed for better alignment or integration with related management systems within the organization (for example, ISO 9001 and ISO 14001).

---

[5] *www.itgovernanceusa.com/shop/product/it-governance-an-international-guide-to-data-security-and-iso27001iso27002-sixth-edition*

Note also ISO 27001:2013 allows an implementation project to address the requirements of the standard in any order—it specifically says the sequence of the clauses should not be taken as setting out implementation precedence. However, starting at the beginning is still a very practical approach.

Structured approach to implementation

A structured ISMS implementation plan should follow the nine steps described in this book. The elements below should all be addressed in the detailed implementation planning:

- Set up your implementation project and project mandate, select a continual improvement model and determine your approach to documentation, set up the management framework, define the internal and external context of the organization, identify the requirements of any interested parties and, taking these issues into account, define the scope of the ISMS.

- Obtain top management commitment to the ISMS, define an information security policy, and allocate roles and responsibilities—including a role responsible for reporting on the performance of the ISMS.

- Define a systematic approach to risk assessment and the risk acceptance criteria.

- Carry out a risk assessment to identify, within the context of the policy and ISMS scope, the important information assets of the organization and the risks to them. This is where you assess the risks.

- Identify and evaluate options for the treatment of these risks, selecting the control objectives and controls to be implemented where required.

- Prepare a Statement of Applicability (SoA) and a Risk Treatment Plan.
- Implement the Risk Treatment Plan and planned controls.
- Provide appropriate training for affected staff, as well as staff awareness programs.
- Manage operations and resources in line with the ISMS.
- Implement procedures that enable prompt detection of, and response to, security incidents.
- Implement procedures for monitoring, reviewing, testing, and audit.
- Implement procedures for reviewing the ISMS and the outcomes of testing and audits in light of a changing risk environment, new technology, or other circumstances. Improvements to the ISMS should be identified, documented, and implemented.

Phased approach

In large, complex organizations, it might be practical to seek multiple certifications, one for each discrete part of the organization, on the basis this minimizes the project complexity and allows for a phased approach to implementation. Where it really is possible to adequately define a scope for a subsidiary part of the organization (and we'll deal more fully with scope as part of the management framework later), such that its information security needs can be independently assessed, it may be possible to gain substantial experience in designing and implementing an ISMS plus a track record of success and the momentum that accompanies it. This may mean a subsequent roll-out to the rest of the organization is carried through successfully and smoothly. These considerations apply to any large, complex project and the appropriate answer depends very much on individual organizational circumstances.

While there are significant benefits to this step-by-step approach, they will all be lost if scoping attempts to create 'artificial' business units, as these will not be accepted by external certification auditors.

The project plan

Normal project planning tools should be deployed in creating and managing the ISMS project. The plan should reflect the high-level timeline contained in the project mandate, be prepared by the project team, and—once it has been critically tested by the CEO and top management—be approved by the board of directors. Senior and top management should be able to understand the plan quickly and easily; to aid this, it should not run to more than two sides of A4. It should also provide sufficient scope for those responsible for its implementation to find appropriate solutions to the many operational challenges that will arise. In other words, it should not be overly detailed—although the thinking behind it should be thorough.

A key preliminary step in any successful change program is to identify and isolate, or convert, potential opposition. Where an ISMS roll-out is concerned, there is sometimes internal resistance from within the IT department. There are a number of possible reasons for this, including the desire of the IT team not to lose control of IT security (particularly where ISO 27001 certification has been set as an IT department responsibility), the IT department's desire to maintain its mystique, and the fear its existing controls might be found to be inadequate. This is not surprising. ISO 27001 does require the organization's top management to take control of its ISMS and the whole organization to get behind and understand key aspects of security policy. The resistance of the IT department can sometimes be expected and must be overcome at the outset. There are circumstances where this can lead to a change in IT staff, either forced or unforced, and the organization should expect this and prepare appropriate contingency plans.

Integration with existing security management systems

ISO 27001:2013 does not require a sequential approach to the establishment and implementation of an ISMS. In reality, once they realize the scale of the information risks they face, many organizations will want to tackle a number of the necessary tasks in parallel. Certainly, most organizations will come to ISO 27001 with some information security structures and controls already in place and with the question of how to intelligently integrate these with any new ones.

Most organizations that embark on ISO 27001 already have a number of information security measures in place, usually to meet existing contractual, regulatory, or business requirements. We call these the 'baseline controls'; your ISMS project should ensure those controls already in place are adequate and appropriate, and any additional required controls are implemented as quickly as possible.

The SoA will only be complete once all the identified risks have been assessed and the applicability of all the identified controls has been considered and documented. Usually, the SoA is started before any controls are implemented and completed as the final control is put in place.

Quality system integration

Many organizations that tackle ISO 27001 may already have an ISO 9001 certificated quality assurance system in place. ISO 27001 was written within the ISO framework, which is designed to encourage integration of management systems within organizations. The ISMS should be integrated with the quality assurance system to the greatest extent possible. In particular, ISO 27001 Clause 7.5, which deals with documentation and document control records, can (and should) be met by applying any existing documentation control requirements of an existing ISO 9000 management system. Procedures and other documents within the ISMS must be controlled. The logical decision for any organization that implements an ISMS is to adopt the ISO 9000 approach.

Effectively, therefore, you could *extend* an existing management system to include information security management, rather than bring in a whole new system. This is an important message that should underpin the organization's change management and communication plans; the smaller the perceived mountain, the more quickly an organization will set out to climb it.

In circumstances where the organization does not already have an existing ISO 9001 certified management system and wants guidance on the documentation, document control, and records issues of ISO 27001, it should obtain and use the guidance in any current manual on the implementation of ISO 9001.

It is also important for the assessment and certification body chosen by the organization to understand and accept this integrated approach. If it does not, get a new one; the task of having the existing system re-assessed (and only at the next planned surveillance date) is much smaller than the task of creating and implementing a wholly new and parallel ISMS.

Looking ahead

The project team should put in place a communications strategy with respect to both internal and external audiences—potentially including stakeholders and stockholders, partners, regulatory bodies, customers, suppliers, etc.—and a staff awareness policy. They will also want to identify what competencies and skills the organization will need in order to address its information security objectives. These two items, to which I will return in due course, should be on the project agenda right from the start.

Costs and project monitoring

The PID contains the approved project budget and high-level project plan. It is the responsibility of project managers to collate and review data about progress and budget utilization, as well as the effectiveness of project risk management measures. The board (or, in a dual-level project structure, the steering group) should review this information on a regular basis, as part of its regular business project review.

The review dates mandated by the board can evolve over time into ISMS review dates, at which point frequency might shift from monthly to annually.

The key points at which to perform a project progress review are:

- After planned completion of each of the nine steps.

- After completion of the draft SoA. Any costs incurred prior to this should be minimal, but until the SoA defines what needs to be done, it will not be possible to budget effectively for the implementation.

- After implementation of the initial suite of procedures that put in place the management framework (discussed later in this book).

- After completion of the first cycle of system audits and reviews and prior to the initial visit by the certification body.

- Annually, as part of the regular review of the ISMS, to ensure the budget is being correctly applied and any new technology issues, risk, threats, or vulnerabilities have been identified and taken care of.

Risk register

The project team, at the outset, should identify the risks to the success of the project. While these typically arise from internal issues—a traditionally open and insecure culture, inadequate management commitment, inadequate project or information security resources, competing demand for resource time and effort, etc.—they may also be triggered by external issues, such as upcoming changes to data protection regulations or security demands triggered by specific clients.

These risks should be listed in the project risk register. Each risk should have an owner, and there should be a plan to mitigate each of the risks by reducing likelihood and/or impact. The project team should review its identified risks, and the effectiveness of its risk management plans, on a regular basis. This key process can make a substantial difference to the effective implementation of the ISMS project plan.

CHAPTER 3: ISMS INITIATION

The first concrete steps in initiating the information security management system (ISMS) are to determine which continual improvement methodology to use and to put a document structure in place.

Continual improvement

ISO 27001 recognizes a 'process approach' is the most effective method for managing information security. The Standard is open to the deployment of any continual improvement approach and allows for organizations that already use, for instance, the ITIL® 7 Step Continual Service Improvement approach, the COBIT® Continual Improvement Life Cycle, or any other approach that may be appropriate in the organization's context, to be certified. One of the most widely known and widely used approaches in the management system world is the 'Plan–Do–Check–Act' (PDCA) model, which will be familiar to quality and business managers everywhere.

Whichever continual improvement model the organization selects, it should be understood before work starts and should inform every step. It should have the idea of root cause analysis (RCA) built or added into it; RCA contributes to identifying whether or not similar issues exist, or could potentially exist, elsewhere in the ISMS and this will enhance the effectiveness of the process—not only for nonconformities (as required by the Standard), but for all issues requiring correction and corrective action.

A common RCA technique is the '5 Whys'. This is a technique for determining the root cause of a problem or defect by repeating the question 'Why?' five times. Each question forms the basis of the next question. While a sixth or seventh iteration might sometimes be necessary, the objective of the technique is to ensure assumptions are questioned and the real root cause of a problem is identified so it can be addressed.

Security improvement plan

I earlier identified that the ISO 27001 project could take the form of a security improvement plan, using a gap analysis as the starting point. Clearly, if this is the route you take, you will want to determine your continual improvement methodology early and ensure you report progress through your continual improvement log.

Expanding the RACI matrix

At this stage, you will also want to expand the RACI matrix by identifying who is formally accountable for the most important roles in the ISMS at the outset.

The roles that need to be identified are the owners of:

- Oversight of the establishment, implementation, operation, maintenance, and improvement of the ISMS
- Continual improvement
- Information security risk assessment, and
- Managing information security incidents.

Documentation

Your risk assessment process determines the controls that must be deployed in your ISMS, and your Statement of Applicability (SoA) identifies the controls you deploy in the light of your approach to risk management. Every one of those controls, together with your approach to identifying and managing risk, your management structure, your decision-making processes, and every other component of your ISMS must be documented as a point of reference; as the basis for ensuring there is consistent application over time; and to enable continual improvement.

Documentation will be the most time-consuming part of the total project; therefore, how you address this aspect will be a major determinant of your overall success. Documentation must be complete, comprehensive, in line with the requirements of the Standard, and should fit your organization like a glove. A properly managed ISMS will be fully documented. ISO 27001 describes the minimum documentation that should be included in the ISMS; i.e., what the organization needs to meet the Standard's requirement to maintain sufficient records to demonstrate compliance.

The key qualities of the ISMS documentation are it should be adequate, but not excessive, and it enables each of the processes to be "systematically communicated, understood, executed and effective so as to be repeatable and dependable."

The documents include:

- The information security policy, the scope statement for the ISMS, the risk assessment, the various control objectives, the SoA and the Risk Treatment Plan. The scope of the ISMS (the minutes of board and steering committee meetings endorsing this can also be helpful).

- The management framework documentation (see the next chapter).

- The underpinning, documented procedures (which should include responsibilities and required actions) that implement specific controls. A procedure describes who has to do what, under what conditions, or by when. These procedures (there would likely be one for each of the implemented controls) would be part of the policy manual that itself can be on paper or electronic.

- Documents that deal with how the ISMS is monitored, reviewed, and continually improved, including measuring progress toward the information security objectives.

All formal documentation should be controlled and available to all staff entitled to view it. It can be published in paper form but is most effective on an intranet, a shared drive, or SharePoint. A shared drive or SharePoint ensures the current version of any procedure is immediately available hassle-free to all members of staff. A structured numbering system should be adopted that ensures ease of navigation of the documentation, controlled document issue, tracking of replacement pages and changes, and completeness of documentation. Staff should be trained in how to use the documentation and how to draft operations procedures for the assets and processes for which they are personally responsible.

Clearly, there will be a number of security system documents subject to security measures. These will include documents such as the risk assessment, the Risk Treatment Plan and the SoA, which contain important insights into how security is managed and should therefore be classified, restricted, and treated in accordance with the organization's information classification system. Access should be limited to people with specified ISMS roles, such as the information security adviser.

Four levels of documentation

ISO 27001 clearly recognizes there is no such thing as a 'one size fits all' approach to documentation. Instead, it recommends the extent of the ISMS documentation should reflect the complexity of the organization and its security requirements. In practical terms, there are four levels of documentation in an ISMS, and each level has different characteristics, including about who is entitled to make decisions regarding revisions to the documents. The four levels are:

1. The approved corporate policy, which drives all other aspects of the ISMS. A number of additional, subject-specific policies support this high-level policy (for instance, setting out what constitutes acceptable use of the Internet).

2. Detailed procedures that describe who is responsible for doing what, when, and in what order.

3. Operations/work instructions that set out in detail precisely how to perform each of the identified tasks.

4. Records, which provide evidence as to what was done.

The amount of work increases as you descend the four levels—once, of course, those are brought into line with the control requirements. The most demanding, in terms of time, is producing the third level—even though this is essentially the documentation of existing ways of carrying out specific activities.

Documentation approaches

There are three approaches to tackling the documentation requirements of the Standard: two traditional and one using a documentation toolkit. In an organization that meets the criteria described earlier in this book, the length of time the project will require depends very much on the methodology adopted.

Trial and error

The first is a methodology known as 'trial and error.' Because those charged with deploying the ISMS first have to learn how to perform every single aspect of the task, it is the most time-consuming of the three, has a high risk of failure, and extends the period during which the organization continues to fail to meet its information security objectives.

External expertise

The second, equally traditional, method is to bring in outside expertise in the form of experienced consultants to produce your documentation. It is a quicker approach than trial and error, but substantially more expensive. Its major advantages include considerably reducing project time, reducing the risk of failure, increasing the speed of organizational learning, and overcoming resource deficiencies.

Third-party documentation toolkit plus guidance

While this approach is most appropriate for organizations that prefer to tackle internal change projects largely without external consultant support, it is an approach the success of which depends as much on the quality and extent of senior management support and commitment as it does on the quality of the tools themselves.

The major advantages of this approach are that documentation toolkits:

- Are fit for purpose—designed to meet ISO 27001 requirements from the outset

- Are fast to deploy

- Are very cost-effective (with low TCO and high ROI)

- Generate substantial cost savings in comparison to traditional approaches

- Are full of best practice

- Will be cross-functional, company-wide, with a correct continual improvement cycle

- Create a very low likelihood of project failure

- Have continuous improvement built in right from the start.

It is essential any documentation toolkit is designed to meet the detailed requirements of the Standard, and comes with detailed guidance on how to tackle the project and all of the detailed drafting requirements. At IT Governance, we designed and built a documentation toolkit that exactly meets the requirements of the Standard, reflects multiple successful deployments of certifiable information security management systems, and was developed specifically for organizations that want to avoid the costs and disadvantages of learning by trial and error. These toolkits are also specifically designed so they can easily be integrated into additional management systems, ensuring the opportunity to build an integrated management system that meets multiple standards is available from the outset.

There is a free trial version of this toolkit available for download through each of our websites. It is worth checking out this toolkit as part of your preparatory research into how you will deal with the documentation part of your project.

Third-party documentation

As part of the documentation processes, controls should also be introduced for documents of external origin, including managing their retention periods.

CHAPTER 4: MANAGEMENT FRAMEWORK

ISO 27001 is a specification for an information security *management* system (ISMS). Unsurprisingly, therefore, it sets out requirements for a management framework. The fourth step in ISMS implementation is to create this framework.

Clause 4 of ISO 27001 says the organization must identify the needs and expectations of interested parties, as well as the internal context of the organization, and these should be taken into account in establishing the scope of the ISMS.

You started to identify these requirements when creating your project risk register, so you should revisit this information and build on it. The external context will include the business and risk environment, what is going on in your sector, and any other developments that might impact your information security stance. The internal context is the range of internal issues that will affect how you design and deploy the management system. In effect, the Standard is saying you must design your ISMS for your business.

As part of this internal context, you will want to begin identifying the organization's risk appetite. This will be a significant issue in many aspects of implementation and I will return to it later in this book.

The requirements of interested parties are more complex. Interested parties can include regulators, partners, and customers. The Payment Card Industry Data Security Standard (PCI DSS), for instance, is a commercial requirement imposed by an acquiring bank; data protection activities are imposed by law and policed by regulators. All organizations face a multitude of such compliance requirements, each of which impose a specific set of information security controls and brings important variations in requirements for preserving confidentiality, integrity, and availability.

The IT Governance Compliance Manager[6] is a tool designed to provide guidance on relevant laws and regulations, identifying the specific clauses that impose compliance requirements and allowing for the addition of multiple third-party contracts that bring their own specific needs.

All these compliance requirements will need to feed into your ISMS, your risk assessment, and your risk treatment documentation. Although the Standard does not require it, it is worth documenting all these aspects for ease of reference and review in future.

As part of documenting the organization's context, it makes sense to review and (re)confirm the information security objectives first documented in the project initiation document (PID) and then further developed when initiating the project.

Scoping

Scoping is fundamentally important. Your management system scope will be stated on your compliance certificate. It will inform the audit as well as the external parties who are interested in your ISMS. It is key, both because you need to know the boundaries of what you are planning to implement, and because the Standard itself requires it. One way of

---

[6] *www.itgovernanceusa.com/shop/product/compliance-manager*

thinking about scoping is from the perspective of your information security policy.

Clause 5.2 of ISO 27001 clearly sets out the requirements with respect to the ISMS policy. The policy must be approved by top management. The policy must provide an overall sense of information security direction for the organization, as well as including information security objectives. It must include meeting information security requirements (which may be business, contractual, or regulatory in nature), and it also must contain a commitment to continually improve the ISMS.

The ISMS policy applies across all parts of the organization that are within the scope of the ISMS. As I said, the scope must take into account the characteristics of the business, its organization, location, assets, and technology—what the Standard calls the "external and internal context" of the organization. ISO 27001 refers, at this point, to ISO 31000: the international best-practice Standard for organizational risk management. For those organizations seeking properly to integrate risk management across all aspects of the business, this ISO 31000 link will be important.

Your policy requirements should drive your approach to scoping the ISMS and the project. Scope determination is harder for larger, more complex organizations than it is for smaller ones. Scoping is essential though for any size of business: you must decide which information assets you're going to protect and which ones you're not before you can decide on appropriate protection.

This should be a quick decision for a small to medium-sized enterprise: the whole organization. That is because there likely will be hard-wired connections between all the information systems and day-to-day working relationships within the business that make it either extremely difficult or impractical to try to segregate one part of the business from another. The notion of segregation is at the heart of effective scoping: ultimately, you will want to try to create an impregnable barrier between the part of your business that is within the scope of your project and everything else. You must be categorical about what is inside your information stockade and what is outside, and this means you don't want *any* information systems, devices, or business units that are both inside *and* outside—because that will be your weakest link.

ISO 27001 explicitly requires you to consider "interfaces and dependencies between activities performed by the organization, and those that are performed by other organizations." In other words, you must identify what is outside the scope of your ISMS, be prepared to justify its exclusion, and manage the associated risks appropriately. This is to help ensure you don't try to draw the boundaries too narrowly.

Endpoint security

In today's business environment, your defensive barrier has to operate at the individual device level and is highly dependent on user compliance with business procedures. In other words, your scoping decision needs to include all the information devices people use in their jobs—such as smartphones, wireless laptops, home offices, etc.—as well as the more obvious central office systems like accounting, payment processing, production, sales and order management, email, office automation, etc. There also may be cloud-based components to take into account.

In larger, more complex businesses, you also will want to ensure the entity within scope has a clearly defined legal and management structure, and there is alignment with the compliance requirements. Part of the reason for your information security system is to ensure you are compliant with myriad laws and regulations, so it makes sense for the entity that has those compliance obligations to be fully within the scope of your information security project.

In other words, those parts of the organization to which your ISMS applies must be clearly identified. Keep in mind an ISMS is a management system, a formal structure management deploys to ensure its policy in information security is applied consistently throughout the organization for which that management is accountable. Scoping of the ISMS therefore may be done on the basis of corporate, divisional, or management structure, or on the basis of geographic location.

A virtual organization, or a dispersed, multi-site operation, may have different security issues than one located on a single site. In practical terms, a security policy and ISMS that encompasses all of the activities within a specific entity for which a specific top management team is responsible is more easily implemented than one that is to be applied to only part of the entity.

It is important to ensure the top management team that is implementing the policy does actually have adequate control over the organization specified within the scope of the information security policy it will be expected to approve, and that it will be able to give a clear mandate to its management team to implement it within that entity. In other words, it is essential to decide the boundary within which protection is to be provided and ensure the team involved has the power to provide it.

Defining boundaries

The business environment and Internet are each so huge and diverse it is necessary to draw a boundary between what is within the organization and what is outside. In simple terms, boundaries are physically or logically identifiable. Boundaries must be identified in terms of the organization—or part of the organization—that is to be protected, which networks and which data, and at which geographic locations.

The organization within the scope must be capable of physical and/or logical separation from third parties and from other organizations within a larger group. While this does not exclude third-party contractors, it does make it practically very difficult (though not necessarily impossible) to put an ISMS in place within an undifferentiated organization that shares significant network and/or information assets or geographic locations. A division of a larger organization that, for instance, shares a group head office and head office functions with other divisions could not practically implement a meaningful ISMS. Usually, the smallest organizational entity capable of implementing an ISMS is one that is self-contained. It will have its own top management team, its own functional support, its own premises, and its own IT network, or will have IT services supplied by a group or other supplier, subject to some form of service level agreement.

It is not unusual for divisions of larger organizations to pursue certification independently. The critical factor is the extent to which they can practically differentiate themselves and their business and information systems from other divisions of the same parent organization.

For larger—usually highly decentralized—organizations that have a multiplicity of systems and cultures, and an extensive geographic spread, it is often simpler as a general rule to tackle ISO 27001 and risk assessment on the basis of smaller business units that meet the general description set out above. Larger, more centralized organizations that have a single business culture and largely common business and information systems throughout are probably better off creating a single ISMS.

If there are aspects of the organization's activities or systems that are to be excluded from the requirements of the security policy, it is critical these are clearly identified—and explained—at the scoping stage. Multi-site or virtual organizations will need to consider carefully the different security requirements of their different sites and their management implications. There should be clear boundaries ("defined in terms of the characteristics of the organization, its location, assets, and technology") within which the security policy and ISMS will apply. Any exclusions should be openly debated by top management and the steering group, and the minutes should set out how and why the final scoping decision was taken.

It could be that, in fact, it is not be possible to exclude from the scope divisions of the organization, components of the information system, or specific assets, either because they are already so integral to it or because their exclusion might have the effect of undermining the information security objectives themselves. Therefore, it must be clear any exclusions do not in any way undermine the security of the organization implementing the ISMS.

For an ISMS certification, auditors are required to assess how management applies its information security policy across the whole of the organization that is defined as being within the scope of the policy. You should expect them to test the boundaries of the stated scope to their limits to ensure all interdependencies and points of weakness have been identified and adequately dealt with.

In reality, as stated earlier, the process of designing and implementing an effective ISMS may be made simpler by including the entire organization for which the board has responsibility.

Network mapping

It can help (but is not essential) to make a network map that shows how your central management and information systems link together and which identifies all of the points at which the outside world can interact with your network. This map will be very simple for a small organization (because the network is simple) and far more complex for a larger, more complex organization. The map you draw to aid your initial scoping exercise will need to be extended as part of the detailed project planning phase to ensure all aspects of your information systems are identified. You do not need a detailed initial map; you just need to know how you will get from the initial one to the detailed one.

There is a range of network mapping software that will automatically map your network for you, some of which has additional helpful management features. The benefit of using such a tool is it will quickly, completely, and competently identify how your network is structured, what types of services are running, and what access points and devices there actually are. A status report of what is actually happening is much more useful than relying on a theoretical map.

Network maps are often drawn using software tools such as SmartDraw and Microsoft Visio, although you can start with a whiteboard and hand-draw a network diagram before attempting to model it with a software tool. Your network map will ultimately need to identify in detail all the devices (e.g., workstations 43, servers 6) connected to it, as well as their functions (e.g., print and file server, domain controller).

Cutting corners

All our experience teaches us it is a mistake to define the scope too narrowly. By 'too narrowly' I mean a scope that, for instance, includes only a head office, or only that bit of the organization that is under pressure from third-party (usually government) funders or customers to become certified. While it may appear on the surface this is a route to a quick and easy certification, it is often in fact a route to a worthless certificate.

In the long run, any external party assessing the nature of an organization's ISMS will want to be sure all the critical functions that may affect its relationship are included, and a limited scope will not do this. We are aware some certification organizations are prepared to consider scopes that cover less than a complete business unit, and, in our opinion, they are doing a disservice to their clients as well as to the integrity of the ISO 27001 schemes. Do not be tempted to use such certification bodies.

In conclusion, I recognize that scoping the ISMS can be very difficult in large, complex organizations. It is certainly an area where experienced, professional support can be helpful in assessing the best way forward, although I would recommend only using consultants who adopt much of the approach set out in this chapter. This is important because the wrong scoping decision can, in the long run, invalidate the certificate you do achieve, and leave key parts of your organization open to all the risks you are attempting to exclude. It will prove far more expensive when you finally focus on the need to do the job properly than if you'd done it right in the first place. Worse, because you did it wrong first time, it will be far harder to get adequate commitment and support for an extended project across the organization than it would have been if you'd sold the whole project to the organization right from the start.

Formalize key arrangements

At this point, you should formalize:

- How you will demonstrate leadership and commitment (all the requirements of Clause 5.1 in the Standard, building on the project mandate).

- The final version of the information security policy.

- The first full version of the RACI matrix, setting out organizational roles, responsibilities, and authorities.

- The communication policy that identifies who communicates with which audiences, when, and through which means. The communications process should include a method to ensure correct receipt and understanding of the message(s) in question.

- The competence requirements for the generic ISMS roles, such as top management, risk owner, internal auditor, etc., as well as those identified when initiating the project and the ISMS. Keep in mind you will also need competent individuals who can implement and maintain the selected information security controls, plus people who can deal with IT security, physical security, and legal compliance. At least one member of the project team, ideally the project manager, should be required to have something like the IBITGQ CIS LI certificate.

You must ensure you have adequate resources to achieve the ISMS objectives.

Information security policy

The information security policy is the main driving force for the ISMS. It sets out top management policy on, and requirements with respect to, information security. It should be a short document, but it must capture top management requirements and organizational reality while meeting the requirements of the Standard. There is a full discussion of the issues involved in, and development process required for, an information security policy statement in *IT Governance – An International Guide to Data Security and ISO27001/ISO27002, Sixth Edition*[7].

Top management must be completely behind and committed to the ISMS; therefore, the policy statement must be issued under their authority and there should be clear evidence, in the form of written minutes, that the policy was debated and agreed by top management and/or by the management steering group. Any revisions to the policy should also be agreed through the same route.

---

[7] *www.itgovernanceusa.com/shop/product/it-governance-an-international-guide-to-data-security-and-iso27001iso27002-sixth-edition*

It will also require participation by all employees in the organization and may require participation from customers, suppliers, stockholders, and other third parties. This is part of the context of the ISMS referred to earlier. In thinking through the security policy, top management and the forum will need to consider how it will impact these constituents and/or audiences, and the benefits and disadvantages the business will experience as a result of this. It is a good idea to start thinking these issues through before you commence the detailed process of designing and deploying your ISMS.

Communication strategy

Communication is important to ISO 27001 project success. Underlying every successful change management program, and especially necessary for the successful roll out of an ISMS, is a well-designed and effectively implemented internal communications plan. Compliance with ISO 27001 and common sense both suggest key components of this plan must include:

- Top-down communication of the information security vision—why the ISMS is necessary, what the organization's legal responsibilities are, what the business will look like when the program is complete, and what benefits it will bring to everyone in the organization.

- Regular cascade briefings to all staff on progress against implementation plan objectives. These briefings should quickly become part of the existing organizational briefing cycle so ISMS progress becomes part of the normal business process—'just another thing we're doing.'

- A mechanism for ensuring key constituencies and individuals within the business are consulted and involved in the development of key components of the system. This ensures they buy into the outcome and to its implementation, and is a key reason for structuring the steering group and project team as suggested in chapter 2.

- A mechanism for ensuring regular and immediate feedback from people in the organization—or in affected third-party organizations—so their direct experience of the initial system as it is implemented can be used in the evolution of the final version. This can form part of your continuous improvement process and, more immediately, offer evidence of effective 'checking.'

These face-to-face communications should be underpinned with an effective information sharing system. Usually, this will be part of the corporate intranet, on which regular progress reports as well as detailed information on specific aspects of the ISMS are posted. Email alerts can tell staff to access the intranet for new information whenever it is posted and the site can encourage feedback by means of a 'write to the CEO' function.

Of course, if the organization does not currently have a well-developed internal communication process, it will need to develop one. Allowance should be made in the outline project planning timetable and resource allocation for the development of such a system. Do not try to take an ISMS project forward without an adequate internal communication process: information security controls depend to a very large extent on the informed and committed behavior of individuals within the organization and, as a result, you simply have to ensure you can deliver this.

Staff buy-in

The initial staff briefing—the one that accompanies the project kickoff—should set out clearly the nature of the threats faced by the organization and the possible costs, in both financial and non-financial terms, of information security breaches. *The Case for ISO27001:2013*[8] and the chapters on information security risk and governance in *IT Governance – An International Guide to Data Security and ISO27001/ISO27002, Sixth Edition*[9] provide useful information that can underpin a communications strategy.

Wherever possible, you should seek local and/or industry-specific information to use in staff presentations, as this gives immediacy and currency to the possible threats. Illustrations of the possible direct consequences to your own organization should be developed in order to make the situation more relatable and help all those involved to appreciate fully the need for the ISMS.

A key part of getting effective user buy-in is translating information security risks and technology issues into widely and clearly understood *business* ones. Top managements and senior managements understand issues in terms of their impact on the business, and unless those impacts are clearly delineated, clearly credible, and clearly quantified, they are not going to pay them much attention. The same is true of functional and business leaders across the organization

---

[8] *www.itgovernanceusa.com/shop/product/the-case-for-iso-27001-2013-second-edition*
[9] *www.itgovernanceusa.com/shop/product/it-governance-an-international-guide-to-data-security-and-iso27001iso27002-sixth-edition*

whose interest is, if anything, more parochially focused on their own specific issues. The truth is they are less interested in the long-term strategic needs of the organization than they are in achieving the specific sets of goals that drive their own compensation or promotion possibilities.

All this means you not only need to translate the information security imperatives into a small number of credible, quantified, and relevant numbers for top management and senior management, you also need to make the ISMS initiative directly relevant to every single person on whose support you're going to rely. Like all organizational politics, there almost certainly is no single message that will do this job for everyone. You're going to need a single, strong, organization-wide, top-down commitment, supported by a large number of one-on-one, locally focused discussions in which you set out how the ISMS project will specifically improve the business circumstances for each person to whom you talk.

A large part of effective project management is sales skills and a detailed understanding of organizational politics. This is why it can be very hard for an outsider to succeed as project manager in delivering an ISMS project.

CHAPTER 5: BASELINE SECURITY CRITERIA

Step five is a straightforward one. It looks at the information security controls you already have in place, assesses them for adequacy, and incorporates them into your ISMS.

As I said earlier, most organizations will make a number of decisions about risks before even starting the ISO 27001 project (after all, they have been in business for a time, dealing with threats and vulnerabilities for real). They also will have implemented a number of controls in order to comply with statutory, regulatory, or contractual requirements. The organization must decide how it incorporates these existing controls into its ISMS and its risk assessment methodology.

The necessity is to implement controls appropriate for the organization, its information security objectives, and the identified business, legal, regulatory, and contractual requirements. We call these requirements the 'baseline security criteria,' because they create the criteria that determine the information security controls you have to put in place, irrespective of your risk appetite or risk assessment.

Your risk assessment methodology should therefore state clearly that the requirements of interested parties have led the organization to implement specific controls called the 'baseline security controls,' and that these controls are incorporated into the ISMS.

At this point, you should assess whether or not your existing baseline security controls are adequate to meet your compliance requirements. This is best achieved by using a comprehensive tool like the Compliance Manager[10] (which contains a comprehensive and detailed collection of all the potentially applicable laws and regulations to determine whether additional controls are necessary in order to meet all your obligations).

This is also a good time to make an inventory of your customer and partner contracts, to identify any specific information security controls contained therein, and to ensure those controls are implemented within the business.

Sarbanes–Oxley, SEC, and NYDFS cybersecurity regulations, DFAR, FedRAMP, PCI DSS, HIPAA, GLBA, state breach laws, and the EU GDPR are all examples of formal requirements for the implementation of baseline security controls. Your single ISO/IEC 27001 management system should identify and include all the policies, procedures, and controls mandated by these regulations. Certification against the requirements of ISO/IEC 27001 should enable an entity to demonstrate it has taken appropriate action to meet these various requirements.

In addition to these controls, you also have to determine how you handle all the other controls that are already in place—the ones you adopted at some earlier point to meet specific security criteria relevant at that time. You either review them now for adequacy and effectiveness, or you recognize their existence and simply accept them as part of your baseline security control set, focusing your risk assessment on those remaining risks that are not yet appropriately treated. For example, a door is a control, but in assessing the security of a room you recognize the door is already in place and either

---

[10] www.itgovernanceusa.com/shop/product/compliance-manager

consider its adequacy as a control or accept it and focus on other entry routes ('attack vectors').

CHAPTER 6: RISK MANAGEMENT

Risk assessment is at the heart of the information security management system (ISMS). Understanding its significance to the overall process is critical, and is one of the keys to project success. Top management adopts an information security policy because there are a number of significant risks to the availability, confidentiality, and integrity of the organization's information, and it mandates the design and deployment of an ISMS in order to ensure its policy is systematically and comprehensively implemented. Therefore, the policy must reflect top management's assessment of information security risks and opportunities. This does not mean top management needs to carry out a detailed risk assessment itself, but it does need to set out a clear overall approach to risk that can be used to take the ISMS project forward.

The organization needs to determine its criteria for accepting risks and identify the levels of risk it will accept. It is a truism to point out there is a relationship between the levels of risk and reward in any business. Most businesses, particularly those subject to formal corporate governance requirements, will want to be very clear about which risks they will accept and which they will not, the extent to which they will accept risks and how they wish to control them. Management needs to specify its approach, in general and in particular, so the business can be managed within that context.

Information risk is one of a number of risks the organization must control, and, to the greatest extent possible, it should apply a common risk management framework to all the risks it faces.

The starting point for any ISMS project manager's consideration of risk is to embrace the existing risk management function (if there is one) inside the organization in order to understand a) its overall approach to risk, and b) its specific approach to information security risk. If the organization does not have any such formal function, it is imperative to identify the current approach to identifying, assessing, and controlling risk—and those involved in the activity—as quickly as possible. You will need to ensure there is a consistent, organization-wide approach to managing information security risks.

Introduction to risk management

All organizations face risks of one sort or another on a daily basis. Risk management is a discipline for dealing with non-speculative risks—those risks from which *only* a loss can occur. Speculative risks—those from which either a profit *or* a loss can occur—are the subject of the organization's business strategy, whereas non-speculative risks—those risks that can reduce the value of the assets with which the organization undertakes its speculative activity—are (usually) the subject of a risk management plan. These are sometimes called permanent and 'pure' risks, in order to differentiate them from the crisis and speculative types. Usually, the identification of a risk as either speculative or permanent reflects the organization's *risk appetite*.

Risk management plans have four linked objectives, which are to:

1. Eliminate risks
2. Reduce those risks that cannot be eliminated to 'acceptable' levels, and then either

3. Live with them, exercising carefully the controls that keep them 'acceptable', or

4. Transfer them, by means of insurance, to some other organization.

Pure, permanent risks are usually identifiable in economic terms; they have a financially measurable potential impact upon the assets of the organization. Therefore, risk management strategies are usually based on an assessment of the economic benefits the organization can derive from an investment in a particular control. In other words, for every control the organization might implement, the calculation is that the cost of implementation should be outweighed by the economic benefits that derive from—or economic losses that are avoided as a result of—its implementation.

The organization should define its criteria for accepting risks (for example, it might say it will accept any risk the economic impact of which is less than the cost of controlling it) and for controlling risks (for example, it might say any risk that has both a high likelihood and a high impact must be controlled to an identified level, or threshold).

This chapter only provides a brief introduction to—and overview of—risk management. There is more detailed guidance on this process in *An International Guide to Data Security and ISO27001/ISO27002, Sixth Edition*[11].

The ISO 27001 requirement is the risk assessment should take into account both the organization's context (internal and external) as well as the requirements of third parties that might be relevant to, or have an interest in, the organization's

---

[11] *www.itgovernanceusa.com/shop/product/it-governance-an-international-guide-to-data-security-and-iso27001iso27002-sixth-edition*

approach to information security. In other words, the risk assessment must be *business-driven* and must reflect legal, regulatory, and contractual requirements. This is one of the most important ideas in information security: we recommend the business, managed by its board of directors, identifies the threats to assets, vulnerabilities, and impacts on the organization, and should determine the degree of risk it is prepared to accept in the light of its business model, business strategy, and investment criteria.

Baseline security controls

As discussed earlier, step five in the ISMS implementation process is to identify and implement the controls required to meet the organization's legal, regulatory, and contractual obligations (there might be a number of different obligations, depending on the jurisdictions within which it operates). It is also necessary to identify any controls that may be required by customers and suppliers, or other contractual mandates, and to include them in the baseline control set. The *Compliance Manager*[12] is a useful tool; it helps identify specific controls that may be required to control risks arising from a failure to meet legal, regulatory, or contractual obligations.

Risk assessment

Risk assessment is defined in ISO 27000 as a process that combines risk identification, risk analysis, and risk evaluation. Risk identification is the "process of finding, recognizing, and describing risks," risk analysis is the

---

[12] *www.itgovernanceusa.com/shop/product/compliance-manager*

"systematic use of information to estimate risk," and risk evaluation is the "process of comparing the estimated risk against given risk criteria" to determine its significance.

In simpler terms, risk assessment is the systematic and methodical consideration of: a) the realistic likelihood of a risk occurring, and b) the business harm likely to result from any such risks.

The risk assessment should be a formal process. In other words, the process should be planned and the input data, its analysis, and the results should all be recorded. 'Formal' does not mean technical risk assessment tools must be used, although in more complex situations they will likely improve the process and add significant value. The complexity of the risk assessment will depend on the complexity of the organization and of the risks under review. The techniques employed to carry it out should be consistent with this complexity and the level of assurance required by top management.

Five-step risk assessment process

There are five steps to a successful risk assessment.

1. Establish a risk assessment framework
2. Identify risks
3. Analyze risks
4. Evaluate risks
5. Select risk management options

Experienced information security and risk management practitioners know manual risk assessment methods are highly dependent on one or two individuals within the organization, are time-consuming (trial and error) and costly to create, and often suffer from data and process inconsistencies that undermine the integrity and dependability of the results. Therefore, they always will use a purpose-built ISO 27001 risk assessment software tool— one that follows the five steps to successful risk assessment outlined above—in order to achieve their organization's risk management objectives consistently and cost-effectively.

Who conducts the risk assessment?

Unless the organization already has a risk management function staffed by people with training that enables them to carry out risk assessments, it will (depending on the complexity of the organization) need to delegate the responsibility to a lead risk assessor. There are two ways of doing this. The first is to hire an external consultant (or firm of consultants). The second is to train someone internally. The second is preferable in most cases, as the risk assessment will need to be reviewed when circumstances change, and having the expertise in-house enables this to be done cost-effectively. If the organization already has a trained information security adviser, this person could take on the role.

In circumstances where the organization has existing arrangements with external suppliers for risk assessment services, or is in the process of setting up a risk management function or capability (in the context of responding to the requirements of the Turnbull Guidance, or Basel III, perhaps), then it should ensure its information security risk assessment process is included from the outset.

Risk analysis

Qualitative risk analysis is by far the most widely used approach. Risk analysis is a subjective exercise in any environment where returns are derived from taking risks—and it is preferable to be approximately correct, rather than precisely wrong. The risk assessment process should also allow for the possibility of unexpected positive outcomes, or what the Standard calls 'opportunities.' Risks are analyzed in terms of their likelihood of occurrence and their impact if they do. The impact can be either positive or negative. Different organizations have different thresholds for what they consider acceptable—what they can live with—regarding likelihood and impact, and this threshold must be defined in terms of risk acceptance criteria.

Risk workshop

One way to perform the risk assessment (having first defined and documented the risk assessment process) is to hold a risk workshop. The starting point for this workshop is for the lead risk assessor to create a list of relevant risks that compromise the confidentiality, integrity, and availability of information that is within the scope of the management system, and which roles within the organization might own each of those risks.

The risk workshop would be convened and managed by the lead risk assessor and would involve all the risk owners from across the business. The role of the risk workshop is to ensure the list of identified risks (and relevant opportunities) is complete and risk owners have been appropriately assigned, to determine the likelihood and impact of each of the identified risks, and to evaluate those risks against the identified risk acceptance criteria.

Impacts

It is necessary to identify the possible impacts the occurrence of a risk event will have on an information asset's availability, confidentiality, or integrity (impact analysis). These impacts should all, wherever possible, be assigned an estimated monetary value, using a category system (e.g., less than $1k, between $1k and $10k, and so on) that reflects the size of the organization and the total cost (direct and indirect) of the incident.

Next, assess the probability of the event occurring using a classification system such as one time every few years, one time per year, one time every six months, etc. Virus attacks would fall into the 'every day' category.

These steps enable you to identify the level of risk (pragmatically, a low–medium–high classification for the impact and likelihood scales is usually adequate for a smaller organization) and then to conclude, for each risk, and in the light of the controls already in place, whether it is acceptable or if some form of additional control is required.

Controls

Your risk assessment drives your selection of controls over and above those that might fall within what I have called the baseline control set. The key thing to keep in mind about the risk assessment is it is not a one-time exercise. You will need to repeat it on a regular basis, just to check your baseline assessment is still accurate and the controls you deployed are still appropriate. You will need to carry out specific risk assessments on an ongoing basis whenever there is a change in circumstances, in business structure or environment, or in the risk profile. Every decision you make about the controls you are going to deploy must be driven by your risk assessment. Your approach to risk assessment will be a cornerstone of your ISMS. That is why many organizations use risk assessment tools as part of their management system.

Risk assessment tools

Most organizations will want to automate their risk assessment process so this best practice becomes embedded in the organization. This is most easily done by acquiring and using a standard ISO 27001 risk assessment software tool. The benefits of automation show through early on in terms of simplifying the actual risk assessment. The long-term benefits are even greater because of the extent to which automation makes the process of review and maintenance so much more robust.

vsRisk™ is a software tool developed specifically for the automation of ISO 27001 risk assessments. You can read more about vsRisk™ here: _www.vigilantsoftware.co.uk_.

Controls

The risk assessment is at the heart of the ISMS, as the controls adopted by the organization will form a significant part of the completed system. The reality is a significant part of the project time will be invested in designing, deploying, testing, and revising appropriate controls that are intended to meet the identified risks. Therefore, it is important to have an overview of controls.

The concepts of _risks_ and _controls_ are linked and are fundamental to your ISMS. Risk might be defined as the combination of the probability of an event and its consequences. Control is defined in ISO/IEC 27000 as a "means of managing risk." A control includes policies, procedures, guidelines, practices, or organizational structures—these can be of an administrative, technical, management, or legal nature. Please note that information security controls are not simply technical in nature. If they were simply technical, they would fail—if only because no control can implement and maintain itself autonomously.

Nature of controls

All information security controls are made up of a mix of process/procedure, technology, and human activity. For example, looking at the virus and cyber threats that are widely recognized even by boards of directors, ISO 27001 Control A.12.2.1—and common sense—require the implementation of controls against malicious software. When you think about this issue, it is immediately clear you must blend technological controls with procedural ones— neither on its own is adequate. It is also clear malware that corrupts a system is not only a business continuity and reputational issue, it may also corrupt records that need to be retained or make it impossible for an organization to complete or submit required reports on time:

At the same time, ISO 27001 Control A.13.2.3 stipulates information "involved in electronic messaging shall be appropriately protected." Anti-malware software on its own just does not meet a requirement that clearly covers both email and instant messaging. What you need, according to both common sense and ISO 27001, is a mix of technology, process, and correct behavior.

Yes, you need an appropriate software package, one that will ensure incoming viruses, worms, and Trojans are stopped at the perimeter—and spam is filtered out. But it is no good if documents that users have specifically requested from external sources to be sent by email are corrupted by the anti-malware software 'just in case.' For example, we know PDFs sent via an automatic response e-marketer are often nuked by the recipient organization's anti-malware software, and the same document when sent individually to the recipient will pass through with little problem. This sort of software set-up promotes disrespect among its users and a tendency to try to bypass it, potentially with attachments that are really dangerous. Instant messaging has become one of the simplest ways for individuals to circumvent email restrictions and ISO 27001 now expects those risks to be identified and controlled.

End-point security is now also a huge issue. Traditionally, the organizational information security perimeter was easy to define and defend, but with the proliferation of handheld devices, wireless networks, and mobile working, the perimeter has become porous and very hard to defend. Depending on the risk assessment, organizations should look at software that will tackle the risks in handhelds rather than making them difficult to deploy. Wireless networks need to be properly set up—and mobile access should be by means of an appropriately secure connection, like a virtual private network (VPN). This control area will be found to interact with Control A.6.2, which requires the organization to have a formal policy and appropriate controls in place to protect against the risks of working with mobile computing facilities.

Of course, anti-malware software needs to work with the firewall seamlessly. It becomes outdated fast, so you need to have procedures in place to ensure it updates properly. Most organizations do not have a lot of time for testing anti-malware or other updates and fixes. Nevertheless, exploits and attacks have revealed vulnerabilities are now arising faster and faster—rapid deployment of fixes is usually critical, and this can only be achieved if you have the right structures and processes in place.

In addition, your staff need to be trained on what to do when there is an incident—whether that is an email virus, a hoax, or someone uploading something from a USB stick. And when it all goes wrong (as, sooner or later, it inevitably will), you need to have in place ways of keeping the ship afloat while you plug the holes.

Control selection criteria

You should only deploy controls that relate to, and are appropriate and in proportion to, the actual risks you face. While you can choose controls from any source you consider appropriate, ISO 27001:2013 requires you to compare any controls you do select against its own list of the key best-practice controls relating to the whole range of potential risks (many of which your organization may not face). The Standard also requires inclusions and exclusions to be justified.

Controls can be described as 'countermeasures for risks.' Apart from knowingly accepting risks that fall within the (top management-determined) criteria of acceptability, or transferring those risks (through insurance) to others, there are three types of control:

1. Preventative controls, which protect vulnerabilities and make an attack unsuccessful or reduce its impact.
2. Corrective controls, which reduce the effect of an attack.

3. Detective controls, which discover attacks and trigger preventative or corrective controls.

Controls are not implemented irrespective of the cost. No top management should sign off on any ISMS proposal that seeks to remove all risk from the business—the business does, after all, exist within a risk framework and, as the only form of existence that is completely risk-free involves already being dead, there is little point in proposing to control every risk.

It is essential any implemented controls are cost-effective. The principle is the cost of implementing and maintaining a control should be no greater than the identified and quantified cost of the impact of the identified threat (or threats). It is not possible to provide total security against every single risk; the trade-off involves providing effective security against most risks.

No organization should invest in information security technology (hardware or software), or implement information security management processes and procedures, without having carried out an appropriate risk assessment that assures them that:

- The proposed investment (the total cost of the control) is the same as, or less than, the cost of the identified threat's impact
- The risk classification, which takes into account its probability, is appropriate for the proposed investment, and
- The priority of the risk has been considered—i.e., all the risks with higher prioritizations have already been adequately controlled and, therefore, it is now appropriate to invest in controlling this one.

If the organization cannot satisfy itself that the proposed investment meets these criteria, it will be wasting both the money and the time required to implement the control, while leaving itself open to more likely risks and, conceivably, with inadequate resources to respond to such risks when they occur. There is, in other words, a risk associated with not carrying out—and maintaining—an adequate risk assessment.

Statement of applicability

The second most important document in your ISMS—after the information security policy statement itself—is your Statement of Applicability (SoA). The SoA is, in essence, a list of all the controls identified in Annex A of ISO/IEC 27001:2013, together with your statement as to whether or not that control is applied in your organization, the justification for its inclusion or exclusion, a statement as to whether or not the control is required, and whether it has actually been implemented or not. The SoA also includes controls selected from other sources, if you have any.

Risk treatment decisions—accept the risk, reject it, transfer it through insurance, or control it, also described as 'Retain, Avoid, Share, and Modify'—have to be made for each risk on the basis of the organization's pre-determined risk appetite and within the context of the risk assessment framework. Risk treatment decisions must be justified by the risk assessment (recognize the baseline controls required to meet legal, regulatory, and contractual objectives) and each control should be proportionate to the identified risk.

ISO/IEC 27002 has the status of a Code of Practice and it provides detailed guidance on how to implement each of the 114 controls listed in Annex A of ISO/IEC 27001.

The best detailed guidance that exists on the market today, and which tackles the SoA on a control-by-control basis, is *IT Governance – An International Guide to Data Security and ISO27001/ISO27002, Sixth Edition*[13], which was chosen as the Open University's postgraduate text book precisely because of the quality of its coverage of this core component of the ISMS. Whether you're using consultants for your project or not, you will find this book indispensable to your ISMS project.[14]

Risk treatment plan

The next most important document, after the SoA, is the Risk Treatment Plan (RTP). This sets out the steps to take in order to deal with each of the risks you identified in your risk assessment. Those risks you are accepting or rejecting need no further action, other than possibly finding a workaround for those you reject. Those you intend to transfer need to be the subject of negotiations with insurers and/or suppliers. Those you intend to control need action, and your RTP describes those actions: what has to be done, by whom, and by when.

---

[13] *www.itgovernanceusa.com/shop/product/it-governance-an-international-guide-to-data-security-and-iso27001iso27002-sixth-edition*
[14] While I acknowledge I am one of the co-authors of this book, the fact is that there is nothing like it on the market.

CHAPTER 7: IMPLEMENTATION

The seventh of the nine steps deals primarily with the implementation of the Risk Treatment Plan—putting in place the selected information security controls. The technical aspects of control implementation—re-configuring firewalls, implementing boot-level encryption on laptops, segregating networks, meeting DPA or PCI compliance requirements, and so on—all depend in the first instance on the competence of those charged with their implementation.

The focal point of this step is the competence of those in the information security team, as well as of others across the organization who will be responsible for documenting processes, for communicating changed processes and controls across the organization, and for staff awareness, training, and education. At this point, you will also deal with outsourced processes.

Competencies

You will need a process to determine, review, and maintain the competencies necessary to achieve your information security management system (ISMS) objectives. Competence is defined in ISO 27000:2014 as the "ability to apply knowledge and skills to achieve the intended results." But what competencies do you need?

To answer this question, you should conduct a needs analysis, assessing the competencies required for the effective management of the ISMS. The organization must define competence, either in terms of experience or in terms of qualifications. The current reality is there are relatively few people who have meaningful ISO 27001 experience; therefore, organizations tend to default to formal qualifications as a way of determining and assessing competence. We have looked at this previously: information security lead implementer, lead ISMS auditor, and internal ISMS auditor are typical competencies required, and International Board for IT Governance Qualifications (IBITGQ) qualifications in these subjects are typical ways that organizations demonstrate they have acquired what they need.

Information security requires more than just implementation and audit competencies, though. It also requires competence in areas like risk assessment, business continuity, and incident management, as well as in more technical areas like security testing and network security architectures. Qualifications like CISMP, CISSP, CEH, and CISM are becoming more common among information security professionals, but you also need to consider specific qualifications, such as those for managing Microsoft or Cisco security, or PKI infrastructure, for instance.

Once you determine the competencies required for your ISMS, you need to acquire them—either through recruitment, sub-contracting, or, more practically, by having your existing staff get trained and qualified. Public training organizations (such as the training arm of IT Governance Ltd) offer these sorts of training courses and access to the associated exams.

Evidence of competence needs to be retained. The most appropriate place in which to do this is individual HR files.

The 'all persons' requirement

It is a requirement of the Standard that all "persons under the organization's control" are appropriately aware of the information security policy, the ISMS—and their contribution to it—as well as the implications of not conforming with ISMS requirements. The group of persons to whom this applies would logically include—as well as employees—all associates and contractors doing work either on behalf of the organization or within its security perimeter, ranging from cleaners to network support engineers.

While it is relatively straightforward to make this work with respect to staff and direct contractors, it is somewhat harder when dealing with those indirectly contracted to do work under the organization's control. For example, cleaners and network engineers, employed by a third party that has a specific service contract with your organization, could be under your control when on your premises. You need to build into supplier contracts an obligation to ensure their staff comply with this requirement—and then make it possible for them to do so.

Staff awareness

It is also a requirement of the Standard that all staff should receive training in relation to the ISMS and their awareness of the ISMS and information security issues should be maintained over time. This is perfectly sensible; staff can be most organizations' weakest link, and in an era where 'hacking the human' is just one of the standard skill sets of most cyber attackers, the humans on your staff need to be on their guard at all times. Of course, staff can make errors—when inputting data, for instance—that could have outcomes as catastrophic as a major cyber attack.

Practically speaking, this means staff need basic training—typically, when they join the organization—on how the IT systems operate and what their obligations are regarding information security. Most staff should also sign an acceptable use agreement when they join the organization. This document should set out in detail all aspects of the expected behaviors, from password strength to clean desk and clear screen policies, and protection of PII. Initial staff training should, at the very least, cover all the acceptable use requirements, as well as the policies and procedures the user is expected to comply with.

The organization should provide refresher training on a regular basis. This refresher training can cover the same areas as the original training, or it can be varied and updated to reflect a changing risk environment. As your objective is continued compliance with your acceptable use agreement, there is some sense in re-delivering the same core training.

There are three challenges with the traditional way of delivering such training, which usually takes the form of a group session. The first is it is expensive in terms of trainer and staff time. The second is that, invariably, not everyone manages to attend the training—and it is the person who does not attend who is likely to cause a problem. The third is you usually cannot extract evidence from this kind of training that everyone paid attention and learned what they were intended to learn. In legal proceedings, a court may request you to demonstrate a transgressor was actually aware their actions were wrong.

Increasingly, organizations address these challenges through eLearning—staff awareness training delivered online. Typically, a 40-minute staff awareness training course can be delivered cost-effectively and consistently to everyone within an organization within a specific timeframe. As everyone completes the training at a time that suits them, you can ensure everyone does get trained. Everyone gets the same message. And you can attach tests to the training, so you have evidence people learned what they were meant to learn. The most important aspect of online compliance staff awareness training is the extent of the administrative reporting. The interactivity of the course itself is far less important, and this has the benefit that you can usually keep down the cost of delivering this sort of training—either from a cloud provider or through your own in-house learning management system.

IT Governance Ltd is one of a number of organizations that can provide online ISO 27001 staff awareness training to help address this need.

Of course, staff awareness training often dovetails with the organization's communication strategy. Keeping staff up-to-date with information security awareness is, in practical terms, simply building on the initial and repeat core training, and should be fundamental to how you keep staff aware of the dangers of a wide variety of social engineering-type attacks.

Outsourced processes

ISO 27001 specifies outsourced processes must fall within the scope of the ISMS, even though the organization delivering that process is by definition outside the scope. An outsourced process is one where the organization has contracted a third party to manage or operate a service on its behalf, such as desktop support. An outsourced service is not necessarily the same thing as a bought-in service; while you are able to determine how an outsourced service is operated, you have little discretion about bought-in ones.

Processes that fall within the scope of the ISMS must be controlled. Typically, outsourced processes are controlled through some mix of:

- Terms and conditions of contract
- Supplier information security questionnaires
- Mandating and monitoring recognized assurance badges, and/or
- Supplier audits.

CHAPTER 8: MEASURE, MONITOR, AND REVIEW

A useful information security management system (ISMS) is one that helps an organization achieve its information security objectives. Those objectives should be linked to its business, regulatory, and contractual obligations, and should be delegated to appropriate levels within the organization.

ISO 27001 requires the organization "to continually improve the suitability, adequacy, and effectiveness of the ISMS." The corrective action requirements of the Standard are met by an effective ISMS audit plan, competent review of nonconformities (part of the responsibility of the information security manager), the incident response procedures, and the related documentation.

The combination of effective monitoring, measuring, and corrective action processes—together with a formal review process and strong internal audit structure—within the context of an ISMS will enable an organization to start driving continual improvement throughout the organization. (Of course, if the original approach to the ISMS implementation was to structure it as a continual security improvement project, then this concept will already be built into the underlying logic of the ISMS.)

A long-term approach to continual improvement should include measuring the effectiveness of the ISMS and of the processes and controls that have been adopted. ISO 27001 requires effectiveness measurements, and for the results from these to be included in the input to the management review meeting. Clearly, information security as an organizational function needs to be measured against performance targets in just the same way as other parts of the organization. The organization also needs to be able to measure progress toward its corporate security objectives, and this also is a requirement of ISO 27001.

In order to develop a useful set of metrics, an organization will have to identify what to measure, how to measure it, and when to measure it.

Key areas that should be considered for their contribution to the organization's ISMS goals and key objectives should include:

- Effectiveness of identified controls and groups of controls that relate to the most significant risks identified in the risk assessment.

- Effectiveness and cost-effectiveness of the organization's information security awareness, education, and training.

- Extent and effectiveness of vulnerability patching and management.

- Improvement in efficiency generated by access controls and external contracts.

- Effectiveness of the incident handling process.

- Effectiveness of perimeter security and speed of remediation through penetration testing.

Internal audit and testing

ISO 27001 requires organizations to conduct internal audits of the ISMS at planned intervals.

Your ISMS has to work in the real world. You identified risks, you deployed what appear to be appropriate controls, and you want to be sure of two things: first, that the controls work as intended, and second, that when they are overwhelmed (as they will be sooner or later) your emergency counter-measures also work. Your management system, including each and every control, is planned and deployed. The management system and every control are then tested to see if they work according to plan, and the management system and every control are improved in light of that testing.

There are four types of testing that should be considered. The first is internal audit, which involves a trained ISMS auditor following a documented procedure and asking for evidence that what is described in the procedure is what actually happens. As part of your ISMS project, you will need to put a team of trained ISMS internal auditors in place. These people can be drawn from around the business, appropriately trained, and—provided you ensure they never audit any part of the business for which they or their managers are responsible—they will meet your long-term audit team requirements.

The second is a limited 'paper test.' This is an intellectual exercise; it requires more than one person, and also requires familiarity with the vulnerabilities in the asset, the mechanisms of the control, and the mechanisms and makeup of the likely threats. Given this knowledge—that should be both current and experientially and technically based—the effectiveness of controls (such as incident management or business continuity controls) can be logically tested.

The third is a limited, real-life test. This could involve powering down the server room during normal operations to find out whether the APS systems and server shut-down procedures all work as specified, for instance. Real-life tests should not be carried out without first having taken extensive steps to ensure that if something does not work as planned the system can be restored to the point it was at when the test was executed. This type of testing includes penetration testing, which should be carried out by a specialist penetration testing firm and should test both your selected controls and your risk assessment: in other words, you should instruct your penetration tester to try to penetrate your system by methods you haven't identified. You can assess later whether these are threats against which you need to control.

The fourth and final type of test is a large-scale scenario test, most usually used to test major cyber incident and business continuity plans. These tests usually try to telescope the events of several days into a much shorter space of time and require all those who would have roles in the real-life disaster to attempt to perform the required tasks in the role play. These tests require considerable planning and, again, it is a sensible area in which to deploy external, specialist expertise.

You will want to schedule audits and tests so all aspects of your ISMS are covered in the course of a year. You should do this on the basis that some controls need to be tested more regularly than others—carry out a risk assessment to determine the frequency of testing you will require. Your external certification auditors will want to see evidence of your internal audit and testing, the results of this activity, and details of how you used the findings of this activity to improve and tighten your ISMS. You should assume your external certification auditor will want to see evidence of at least one cycle of audits and tests. If you want to achieve certification after less than one year's worth of testing, you will need to design a test and audit cycle that covers all the mission-critical aspects of your ISMS within a much shorter timeframe. This is not an unusual approach and most certification bodies accept there are a number of items that do not need to be tested that regularly.

Management review

Top management should review the performance of the ISMS on at least an annual basis. Inputs to the management review process will include all the results from internal audits and testing, as well as continual improvement activity and analysis of nonconformances and incidents that have occurred during the preceding period. As I said elsewhere, root cause analysis is the preferred approach.

The management review should look inwards at the performance of the management system, and at the metrics that describe how the ISMS is performing in relation to its objectives. It should also look outwards at the world in which the organization operates, to ensure it is taking appropriate steps in the context of changes to its operating and risk environment.

CHAPTER 9: CERTIFICATION

While your selection of certification body should have no impact on your success in achieving certification, there are a couple of issues you should consider in making your selection, which is not necessary until you have made considerable progress toward readiness for certification. Of course, you will want to ensure there is a cultural fit between you and your certification services supplier, and pricing and terms are acceptable.

There are two other key issues that do need to be taken into account when making this selection: the first is relevant to organizations that already have one or more externally certified management systems in place, while the second applies specifically to organizations tackling ISO 27001.

It is essential your ISMS is fully integrated into your organization; it will not work effectively if it is a separate management system and exists outside of and parallel to any other management systems. Logically, this means the framework, processes, and controls of the ISMS must integrate with, for instance, your ISO 9001 quality system to the greatest extent possible. Clearly, therefore, assessment of your management systems must also be integrated: you want one audit that deals with all aspects of your management system. Doing anything else is simply too disruptive to the organization, too costly, and too destructive to good business practice. You should ensure whomever you choose for your ISMS audit can, and does, offer an integrated assessment service.

The second issue you should take into account when selecting your supplier of certification services is their approach to certification itself. An ISMS is fundamentally designed to reflect the organization's assessment of risks in and around information security. In other words, each ISMS will be different. It is important, therefore, that each external assessment of an ISMS takes that difference into account so the client gets an assessment that *adds value* to its business, rather than one that is merely a mechanical comparison of the ISMS against the requirements of ISO 27001.

Once you choose your certification body and are ready for a certification audit, there are six secrets to certification success. None of these secrets will get you through an audit you are fundamentally not ready for, nor will they enable an inadequate ISMS to achieve certification. However, they do ensure all the good aspects of your ISMS are noted and the auditors are left with a favorable overall impression.

1. Impress the auditors as early as possible by ensuring your documentation is complete, comprehensive, and all available for inspection at the initial visit—the one that comes before the actual certification audit. This first visit is expressly to determine if your ISMS is ready for external audit.

2. Ensure all your internal audit and testing records are immediately available for the certification auditors when they plan and commence their work. They will use these records to focus their attention on key areas of the ISMS, so ensure you have adequately tested them. No external auditor wants to sign off on a system that is breached a week later, and the thoroughness of your own work will give the auditor confidence.

3. Teach staff throughout the organization to be completely open and honest with the auditors, especially about things they feel may not be up to standard. This serves

two purposes: it flushes out weaknesses you can tighten up on, and it demonstrates to the auditors that you have an open organization that identifies and deals with information security issues. By contrast, an attempt to suggest everything is perfect throughout the organization will provoke incredulity among the auditors; they have learned, through long experience, that no system is without flaws and every attempt to pretend to perfection hides a myriad of previously undetected imperfections. Do not encourage them to start hunting down these imperfections.

4. Teach staff who are likely to be interviewed by auditors to show how the system that is being examined actually works, and to restrict what they say to answering the specific questions asked without explaining anything off-topic. This will demonstrate to the auditor that your people are tightly focused, and will also avoid the danger of someone talking so much that they lead the auditor to examine an aspect of your ISMS that does not need external examination.

5. Critically, ensure management is fully involved in the certification audit. If necessary, rehearse with senior management the type of questions they will be asked and the type of answers they will be expected to give. While senior management should be perfectly capable of handling the audit (as they will have been involved in and fully committed to the ISMS project from the outset), they may not be fully aware of how best to demonstrate this commitment to an external auditor. If it is strong, senior management's performance on the day can make a substantial contribution to certification success.

6. Be prepared to argue. You should do this only in a constructive and calm fashion, but if there are issues on which you feel an auditor has misunderstood your ISMS or some aspect of it, or has misinterpreted the Standard, and is, as a result, thinking about recording a nonconformity (either major or minor), you should set out, calmly and firmly, why you believe you are in the right. Auditors will respond negatively to any attempt to browbeat or belittle them; they will (usually) respond positively to any constructive attempt to help them achieve a better outcome. And the greater their conviction you're committed to the long-term effectiveness of your ISMS, the more prepared they will be to give you the benefit of the doubt on any marginal decisions.

The outcome of the initial audit should, if the organization has diligently followed all the recommendations contained in this book, be certification of the ISMS to ISO 27001 and the issuing of a certificate setting this out. The certificate should be appropriately displayed and the organization should start preparing for its first surveillance visit, which will take place about six to nine months later. Any minor nonconformances should be capable of being closed out by email, and any recommendation for certification will be dependent on this happening within an agreed timescale.

The certificate will refer to the latest version of the SoA and the auditors will check for updates on their subsequent visits. Therefore, when supplying a copy of the certificate to clients, stakeholders, or other parties, the organization should be prepared to provide a copy of the most recent SoA. While the SoA is a living document, updated as and when necessary, the organization should endeavor to keep such updates and alterations to a minimum.

ISO 27001 RESOURCES

ISO 27001 Cybersecurity Documentation Toolkit

Overview

The ISO 27001 Cybersecurity Documentation Toolkit was developed by leading ISO 27001 experts, compiling real-world practice and experience into easy-to-use document templates.

ISO 27001 Cybersecurity
Documentation Toolkit

This documentation toolkit provides a complete set of easy-to-use, customizable documentation templates that align with ISO 27001, NIST SP 800-53, and the NYDFS Cybersecurity Requirements to save you time and money.

Benefits

- Achieve compliance with a range of information security regulations.
- Accelerate your management system implementation, saving you time and money.
- Know how NIST SP 800-53 maps to ISO 27001:2013.
- Ensure nothing is left out of your ISMS documentation.
- Streamline compliance with ISO 27001:2013, making it easier and simpler for you and your team.
- Reduce the room for error and time-wasting when developing your own templates.
- Block off potential project dead ends.
- Easily integrate your ISMS documentation with your business processes.

Features

- Fully customizable.
- Optional: Integrates with risk assessment tool vsRisk™.
- Provides complete coverage of ISO 27001:2013.
- One-time automation input to handle repeated information.

Download a free toolkit trial here:

www.itgovernanceusa.com/isms-iso27001-documentation-toolkit-demo

vsRisk™

Overview

vsRisk is an information security risk assessment software tool created by ISO 27001 industry-leading experts. Fully aligned with ISO 27001:2013, vsRisk is a desktop tool that allows  you to conduct an information security risk assessment quickly and easily. vsRisk™ simplifies the risk assessment process, cuts costs, and ensures accurate, repeatable risk assessments, year after year.

Benefits

- Save 80% of your time and significantly cut the consultancy costs that are typically associated with tackling a risk assessment.
- Ensure accurate results and enable risk assessments to be repeated year after year.

- Meet ISO 27001 requirements for consistent, valid, and comparable results.
- Accelerate control implementation with the integrated ISMS Documentation Toolkit.
- Generate six audit-ready reports for exporting, editing, and sharing across the business and with auditors— including the SoA and RTP.

Features

- Track risks, actions, and priorities from dashboard views.
- Copy, edit, and replicate a built-in sample risk assessment.
- Upload policies or procedures for controls right from an ISO 27001 documentation toolkit.
- Apply implementation details.
- Collaborate with multiple users or assessors.
- Add comments and deadlines.
- Add or clone additional ISMSs.
- Draw, edit, and print instant audit-ready reports.

View the product details here:

vsRisk Standalone:
www.itgovernanceusa.com/shop/product/vsrisk-standalone-basic

vsRisk Multi-user:
www.itgovernanceusa.com/shop/product/vsrisk-multi-user-full

ISO 27001 Staff Awareness eLearning

Overview

This eLearning course enables employees to gain a better understanding of information security risks and compliance  requirements in line with ISO 27001:2013, thereby reducing the organization's exposure to security threats. Using IT Governance's substantial experience in consulting and training, this course is set out to meet the requirements of ISO 27001:2013, which specifies it is imperative to address security issues at the employee level.

Benefits

- The use of non-technical language ensures all staff understand the content.
- The course provides systematic, consistent, and repeatable training across multiple learners.
- Simple to use with relevant and informative content.
- Enables basic yet fundamental training on information security and ISO 27001:2013, reducing the organization's liability due to security failures.
- Provides comprehensive reports as evidence training has actually been provided.
- Can be deployed for existing employees and as part of an induction process for new hires.

Course overview

- An introduction to information security
- The definition of information security in ten seconds
- A description of seven real-life scenarios

- The benefits of maintaining ISO 27001 compliance
- What is an ISMS and what makes a good ISMS?
- What different risk profiles mean for your organization
- A brief explanation of important ISO 27001 controls
- What does ISO 27001 require an organization to do?
- Information security at work
- Physical security and digital security
- Information protection: Information classification and intellectual property
- Dealing with security incidents and business continuity
- Important documentation

Other Information

The course includes an online test and certificate. The course is customizable upon request, and can be hosted externally (from our online e-hosting learning environment) or internally (from your own network environment).

View the course details here:

www.itgovernanceusa.com/shop/product/information-security-iso27001-staff-awareness-elearning-course

ISO 27001 DIY Packages

IT Governance offers four DIY packages that provide a unique set of specially curated and affordable tools and resources designed to help organizations implement an ISMS aligned with ISO 27001.

DIY package benefits

- Get comprehensive tools and guidance from experts in ISO 27001.
- Take control of your own project by implementing an ISO 27001-compliant ISMS.
- Avoid costly consultancy fees and implement the Standard at a budget.
- Empower yourself and your team to retain the needed skills for implementing ISO 27001.
- Get detailed implementation advice based on practical experience.
- Access all the resources in your own time and at your own pace.
- Use the tools to reduce the time and effort required to implement a management system.

Features

Three international standards, essential as a reference for implementing the Standard:

- The ISO 27001:2013 standard
- The ISO 27002:2013 standard
- The ISO 27000:2014 standard

Two bestselling implementation guides, delivering practical implementation guidance:

- *IT Governance – An International Guide to Data Security and ISO27001/ISO27002*
- *Nine Steps to Success – An ISO 27001 Implementation Overview*

Tools proven to save time and money:

- vsRisk™—the definitive cybersecurity risk assessment tool
- The ISO 27001 Cybersecurity Documentation Toolkit

ISO 27001 Live and Online Training courses
- Three-day ISO 27001 Certified ISMS Lead Implementer Online Masterclass
- Five-day ISO 27001 Certified ISMS Lead Auditor Online Masterclass

Live, Online Consultancy
- Up to 40 hours of online consultancy, delivered by an ISO 27001 implementation specialist, according to a project plan.

	DO IT YOURSELF	GET A LITTLE HELP	GET A LOT OF HELP
Set of 3 standards	✓	✓	✓
2 implementation guides	✓	✓	✓
Policies and procedures toolkit	✓	✓	✓
Risk assessment software	✓	✓	✓

2 training courses and exams	✓	✓	✓
Live Online consultancy		2 hours	Up to 40 hours

View package details here:

www.itgovernanceusa.com/iso27001-solutions

ISO 27001 Certified Foundation Online Training Course

Overview

This one-day course provides a complete introduction to developing an ISMS aligned to the best-practice standard ISO 27001.

This course is delivered live online

Save time and travel costs with training delivered to any location with Internet access.

What will delegates learn?

- An overview of management system standards and integrated management systems
- ISO 27001 and how it improves information security
- Understanding management system documentation and the requirements of ISO 27001

- The drivers for certifying an ISMS and the process of certification
- Key elements of an ISMS implementation project: planning, scoping, and communication
- The key steps of an ISO 27001 risk assessment
- The value of accredited certification
- The ISO 27001 Annex A controls

View further details here:
www.itgovernanceusa.com/shop/product/iso27001-certified-isms-foundation-online

ISO 27001 Certified ISMS Lead Implementer Online Training Course

Overview

This three-day course covers all of the key steps involved in planning, implementing, and maintaining an ISO 27001-compliant ISMS. Delegates who pass the included exam are awarded the ISO 27001 Certified ISMS Lead Implementer (CIS LI)  qualification issued by the International Board for IT Governance Qualifications (IBITGQ).

This course is delivered live online

Save time and travel costs with training delivered to any location with Internet access.

What will delegates learn?

- Securing senior management commitment and building the business case

- The role and structure of an information security policy
- How to determine the scope of your ISMS based on the requirements of ISO 27001
- Developing a management framework
- How to structure and manage your ISO 27001 project
- How to allocate roles and responsibilities for your ISO 27001 implementation
- The definition of risk in ISO 27001 and options for risk assessments under the Standard
- The benefits of, and key issues when selecting, a risk assessment tool
- How to carry out an information security risk assessment—the core competence of information security management
- The Statement of Applicability (SoA), and justifications for inclusions and exclusions
- Reviewing your existing controls and mapping controls to Annex A of ISO 27001
- How to manage and drive continual improvement under ISO 27001
- How to prepare for your ISO 27001 certification audit

View further details here:

www.itgovernanceusa.com/shop/product/iso27001-certified-isms-lead-implementer-online

ISO 27001 Certified ISMS Lead Auditor Online Training Course

Overview

This course will teach attendees how to plan and execute an ISO 27001 information security management system (ISMS) audit. Delegates who pass the included exam are awarded the ISO 27001 Certified ISMS Lead Auditor (CIS LA) qualification issued by the International Board for IT Governance Qualifications (IBITGQ).

This course is delivered live online

Save time and travel costs with training delivered to any location with Internet access.

What will delegates learn?

- Best-practice audit methodology based on ISO 19011
- Preparing, leading, and reporting on the findings of an information security audit
- How to audit an ISMS against ISO 27001
- Interview techniques, following audit trails, and reviewing and documenting evidence
- Audit risk assessments, business continuity, and continual improvement
- Identifying nonconformities and ensuring appropriate corrective action is undertaken
- New audit skills and knowledge, enhanced through role-play exercises, workshops, and case study reviews.

View further details here:

www.itgovernanceusa.com/shop/product/iso27001-certified-isms-lead-auditor-online-masterclass

ISO 27001 Custom Consultancy

Overview

Whatever an organization's ISO/IEC 27001 consultancy needs, IT Governance has the right level of service that will help you successfully implement an ISO 27001-compliant information security management system (ISMS)—100% certification guaranteed.

All of our ISO 27001 consultancy services can be delivered online to reduce consultancy fees and ensure optimal return on investment.

Why thousands of companies trust us for ISO 27001 advice:

- Enjoy the peace of mind that your project is in the hands of the world's ISO 27001 experts.
- Receive a 100% guarantee of successful certification.
- Benefit from pragmatic, proven, and straightforward implementation approach.
- Receive support developing a business case to secure the necessary information security investment.
- Choose from the most exhaustive range of ISO 27001 tools, books, and training courses in the world.
- Use the certification body of your choice—we support independent accredited certification.
- Select the best fit for your needs and objectives—we're independent of vendors and certification bodies.

• Our management standards expertise means we can help with much more than a single project.

Consultancy services

IT Governance delivers the full range of support required to help you achieve ISO 27001 certification, including the following popular services:

• **ISO 27001 Gap Analysis**
This expert, in-person review of your information security arrangements against the requirements of ISO/IEC 27001:2013 is ideal for organizations seeking to develop a business case and secure budget approval for implementing an ISO 27001-aligned ISMS.

• **ISO 27001 FastTrack™**
A fixed-price online consultancy package designed to help small organizations with fewer than 20 staff reach ISO 27001 certification readiness in just three months.

• **ISO 27001 Internal Audit**
Outsource your internal audit to a qualified auditor with deep experience of ISO 27001 and the audit process, and gain the assurance you need to ensure you meet your clients' and stakeholders' demands.

• **ISO 27001 Managed Service**
The annual ISMS Management Service helps you to proactively manage, monitor, and maintain your information security management system (ISMS), ensuring consistent conformity to ISO 27001—for a fixed price.

View further details of our ISO 27001 consultancy services:

www.itgovernanceusa.com/iso27001_consultancy

ITG RESOURCES

IT Governance is a specialist in the field of information security and ISO 27001. We have been involved in designing and successfully implementing cost-effective ISO 27001-compliant information security management systems (ISMSs) since the Standard was first introduced.

We are unique in our ability to provide everything you need in order to implement a best-practice ISMS with the minimum of disruption and difficulty, including standards, tools, books, training, and consultancy and support as detailed in the *ISO 27001 Resources* section.

Publishing services

IT Governance Publishing (ITGP) is the world's leading IT–GRC publishing imprint that is wholly owned by IT Governance Ltd.

With books and tools covering all IT governance, risk, and compliance frameworks, we are the publisher of choice for authors and distributors alike, producing unique and practical publications of the highest quality, in the latest formats available, which readers will find invaluable.

You can find more information on the dedicated ITGP website: *www.itgovernancepublishing.co.uk*.

Other titles published by ITGP that may be of interest include:

* IT Governance – An International Guide to Data Security and ISO27001/ISO27002
  www.itgovernanceusa.com/shop/product/it-governance-an-international-guide-to-data-security-and-iso27001iso27002-sixth-edition

- Information Security – A Practical Guide
  www.itgovernanceusa.com/shop/product/information-security-a-practical-guide-bridging-the-gap-between-it-and-management

- The Case for ISO 27001 (2013), Second Edition
  www.itgovernanceusa.com/shop/product/the-case-for-iso-27001-2013-second-edition

We also offer a range of toolkits that provide organizations with comprehensive and customizable documents to help create the specific documentation required to properly implement management systems or standards. Written by experienced practitioners and based on the latest best practice, ITGP toolkits can save months of work for organizations working toward compliance with a given standard.

Please visit *www.itgovernanceusa.com/iso27001_toolkits* to see our full range of toolkits.

Books and tools published by ITGP are available from all business booksellers and the following websites:

www.itgovernance.eu   *www.itgovernance.co.uk*

www.itgovernance.in   *www.itgovernancesa.co.za*

www.itgovernance.asia   *www.itgovernancegulf.com*

Daily Sentinel newsletter

You can stay up to date with the latest developments across the whole spectrum of IT governance subject matter—including risk management, information security, ITIL and IT service management, project governance, compliance, and so much more—by subscribing to our newsletter.

Simply visit our subscription center and select your preferences: *www.itgovernanceusa.com/daily-sentinel*

EU for product safety is Stephen Evans, The Mill Enterprise Hub, Stagreenan, Drogheda, Co. Louth, A92 CD3D, Ireland. (servicecentre@itgovernance.eu)